A STUDY OF

DEITIES OF RIG VEDA

(With the help of Science)

A STUDY OF
DEITIES OF RIG VEDA
(With the help of Science)

S.S. Gupta

ABHINAV PUBLICATIONS

abhinav publications

NEW DELHI

Cataloging in Publication Data—DK
Courtesy: D.K. Agencies (P) Ltd.
<docinfo@dkagencies.com>

Gupta, Shanti S. (Shanti Swarup), 1929-
A study of deities of Rig Veda : with the help of science / S.S. Gupta.

p. ; cm.

Includes bibliographical references (p.)

ISBN 8170174481

1. Gods, Hindu, in literature. 2. Goddesses, Hindu, in literature. 3. Vedas. Rigveda—Criticism, interpretation, etc. 4. Hinduism and science. I. Title.

DDC 294.521 1 21

First published in India 2006

Publishers
Shakti Malik
Abhinav Publications
E-37 Hauz Khas
New Delhi-110016 (INDIA)
Phones: 26566387, 26562784, 26524658
Fax: 91-11-26857009
e-mail: shakti@nde.vsnl.net.in
website: http://www.abhinavexports.com

ISBN 81-7017-448-1

Phototypesetting in Baskerville 12 pt by
Onkar Digital Studio, Delhi
Printed at
D.K. Fine Art Press Pvt. Ltd., Delhi

Contents

Preface

I was tempted towards the study of Rig Veda because of many reasons. First and foremost was that a Hindu, by nature and prevalent practice, tends more towards *Dharma* after retirement. This was a motivating force for me also due to my family background. Then, per chance, the book, *Hindu Economics,* written by a scholar and known leftist, Dr. M.G. Bakare, came in my hand. A careful reading left me dazed and unconvinced. I could not believe that Hindu scriptures, specially Rig Veda, contain sound principles of economics. I wanted to have a first hand information. Then, I have a vague idea that people with authority have often said and written that the Vedas are the repository of all knowledge. I wanted to know the truth. The reading of works of A.A. Macdonell, A.B. Keith, Max Muller, R.T.H. Griffith, H. Oldenberg, Rudolph Roth, A. Hillbrandt, Dr. Surya Kanta, Maharshi Dayananda Saraswati and a few others (Dr. Lakshman Swaroop, Satvelakar, etc.), in my humble opinion, did not substantiate this very important statement. So I wanted to try myself and see what the truth was.

First reading of Rig Veda, with the help of Hindi translation, did not leave me wiser. But the tenacity in my character forced me to try again. I thought it would be better to be specific. So, I picked up, at random, Indra Devata, one of the most popular Devatas. The studies were rewarding. I was convinced that what the Rishis were saying was not pure imagination but there was a lot of truth—science, arts, philosophy, logic, psychology, sociology, and what not, all rolled in one. A small book on Indra was published. Encouraged, I tried to paint on a wider canvas.

I want to apologise, in the very beginning, for my audacity. I have never been a student of *Sanskrit* and yet I have tried to tread this difficult path on which the established scholars are hesitant to walk. After having read Rig Veda several times with the help of various translations, in English and Hindi, after having consulted a few Vedic Indices and having read works of scholars, I felt I should have my own way. So, first of all I started collecting and systematising matter, topicwise, i.e., Devatawise, with the help of research methods. Then I felt the need of taking help of my worthy colleagues of science, specially teachers of Physics. Slowly, a clearer picture started emerging—very different from that found in scholarly works. The results were so encouraging and different from the prevalent ones that I could not check my temptation of writing. So, I can only say that in this work the mistakes are mine—indicator of my ignorance and so should be excused and the good things, if any, are because of the blessings of Maa Saraswati, the goddess of learning.

At several places, I felt it would have been much better had the Rishis and their pronouncements been arranged in a chronological order. This would have automatically given a proper sequence to the development of the ideas. Unfortunately, this has not been done so far. So, it is possible that some unintentional mistakes might have crept into this work. I, obviously, was not competent enough to arrange these Rishis or their ideas in a chronological order.

There are not many authentic Rig Veda Indices. Most of them have been compiled by the foreigners who, themselves, have admitted of their limitations of language and their different social and cultural background. Then, they are not exhaustive. Moreover, they cover too wide an area—all the Vedas and also thereafter. The Indian scholars have probably not thought it proper to "waste" their time and energy on preparing Indices. The scholarly work like Rig Veda Samhita, Edited by N.S. Sontakke and C.G. Kashikar (Vaidika Samshodhana Mandala, Pune), in spite of the very important lists of Rishis, Devatas and Mantras (with details) given in the end, cannot be called an Index. So, any study, naturally, becomes more difficult in absence of a good Index.

The reading of scholarly works gave me an impression that no efforts have been made to identify the Devatas of Rig Veda. I was convinced that the thirtythree Devatas of Rig Veda should have some interconnection with each other. I also felt the need to identify them in terms of modern knowledge, including science. So, I searched the connecting link. Luckily the idea of five basic elements came handy. A starting was made keeping them in mind. And Lo! Wonder of all wonders! All the thirtythree Devatas gradually got identified and they formed different groups around each main Devata, i.e., basic five elements. The whole knowledge about five basic elements—*Aakaasha* (Sky), *Prithvi* (Earth), *Agni* (Sun), *Vayu* (Air) and *Varuna* (Water), given by Rishis of Rig Veda, was almost identical with the scientific knowledge of today. So, these Rishis, in their own style, were giving the scientific knowledge. They were describing the natural phenomena, calling them god.

I humbly hope and pray that this small study may persuade scholars to take up more intensive studies with the help of research methodologies and with the help of available knowledge of various subjects. Such studies, I am sure, will change the methodology and topics of researches in Sanskrit and other subjects undertaken in various educational institutions. If this happens, it will be a good day for India and the world.

In this small work references from Rig Veda have been given in brackets. These references have been taken either from the Hindi translations of Rishi Dayananda Saraswati, Delhi or Pt. Shri Ram Sharma, Bareilly and English translations of H.H. Wilson, Delhi or Ralph T.H. Griffith, Delhi.

A good number of friends, belonging to different disciplines and a few librarians have liberally obliged me in a number of ways. One easy way to get away with their obligation is to mention their names here and give them profound thanks.

But will it not be too formal? I honestly feel the correct method should be neither to mention their names nor to give them formal thanks but to remember their kindness and help, silently, during the entire remaining life. It should help in creating and cementing permanent relationships. An Indian poet has rightly said that a dumb enjoys jaggery (Gur) silently. So I wish to try to follow him.

After the study of Natural Phenomena Gods and their associates, I discovered that there are some other gods also. Reading and re-reading about these gods suddenly gave me an idea. I found that some are "Spiritual Gods", some are "Craftsmen Gods" and some are "Miscellaneous Gods".

The photographs of Deities of this book are different from those which are available in the market. The ideas about Deities have been given by the author on the basis of the study of Rig Veda to Dr. (Smt.) Pratiksha Chauhan, who has designed them on computer.

Aligarh S.S. Gupta

BOOK I

Natural Phenomena Gods

— Agni Devata (Energy Gods)

— Surya and Associate Deities

— Aaditya-Gan

— Aakaasha Devata (Sky)

— Prithvi Devata (Earth)

— Varuna Devata (Water)

— Vayu and Associate Deities

Agni Devata (Energy Gods)

Agni Devata is a very important Devata of Rig Veda. However, a study of Rig Veda created lot of confusion. Agni is one of the important five elements—Agni (Fire), Aakaasha (Sky), Prithvi (Earth), Vayu (Air) and Jala (Water), but great importance has been given to Surya Devata. I could find that Surya is light, it is illuminating, it scorches, etc. but nowhere it is said that it is Agni. On the other hand, Rishi Aangirasa is credited with the invention of Agni, which certainly means fire, or Agni on the Prithvi. The fire of the forests is known as *Daavaagni*, which is nothing but fire on earth. References are found rarely and scattered here and there, of Agni below the Prithvi which has been called *Badvaagni*. Then Rishis talk of sky Agni and because it is of a different type, call it *Apaam Napaat* (lightning). Then at another place, mention is made of fire inside the body called *Jatharaagni*. Description of all of these fires gave me an idea that they should be connected with each other. They must be bound with some common factor. So, brooding started. It continued for days and one night, I felt I was awake and yet dreaming. Dream revealed that *Agni* is a wider term which includes all types of heats such as

1. Agni heat of Surya, i.e., Nuclear Heat
2. Agni on Prithvi
3. Agni below Prithvi
4. Agni above Prithvi
5. Agni in the body

So, *Agni* means heat. This wider term includes all types of heats.

The following pages have been arranged to discuss the various aspects of this mighty *Agni Devata.*

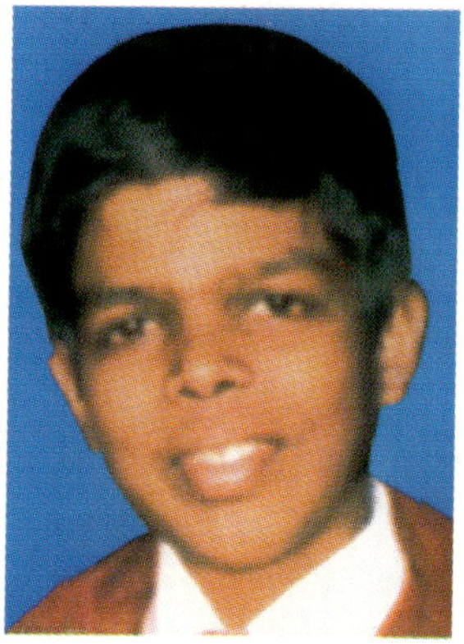

To Dearest
Ashisha
Who had god-like qualities.
Who is no more with us
(left for heavenly abode
on 6.2.2001, at an early
age of 17 years)

Agni Devata

Bhaga Devata

MATA ADITI & MAUSI DITI

Savita Devata

USHA DEVATA

KAZAKHSTAN
MONGOLIA
CHINA
IRAN
IRAQ
EGYPT
SAUDI ARABIA
INDIA

Varun Devata

Ashvini Kumars

Indra Devata

Mitra Devata

Surya Devata

Vayu Devata

Marudga
Devata
Vaa
Deva
MONGOLIA
CHINA
IRAN
INDIA
EGYPT
SAUDI ARABIA
CHAD

Surya and Associate Deities

Chapter 1

Surya Devata

In Rig Veda Surya Devata occupies an important place. It was, therefore, considered essential to collect all Mantras from Rig Veda offered or addressed to Surya Devata. It was thought that this will help in knowing the powers of Surya Devata, his functions and the advantages that he bestows on the human beings. It might also help in identifying him.

The writer started this study with the hypothesis that the Surya Devata of Rig Veda and the Sun of today are one and the same thing.

Important Suktas and Mantras, addressed to Surya Devata are:

	Sukta	*Rishi*	*God*
1.	1.50	Praskadva Kaandava	Surya
2.	1.115	Kutsa Aangirasa	Surya
3.	10.37	Abhitapa Saurya	Surya
4.	10.158	Chakshu Saurya	Surya
5.	10.170	Vibrahaat Saurya	Surya

	Mantra	*Rishi*	*God*
1.	1.164.44	Deerghatamaa Auchathya	Surya, Agni, Vayu
2.	1.164.46	Deerghatamaa Auchathya	Vaak
3.	1.164.47	Deerghatamaa Auchathya	Surya
4.	1.164.51	Deerghatamaa Auchathya	Surya, Parjanya, Agni
5.	1.164.52	Deerghatamaa Auchathya	Surya, Sarasvaan
6.	4.40.3	Vaamdeva	Surya
7.	5.40.5	Atri	Surya
8.	7.60.1	Vasishtha	Surya
9.	7.62.1-3	Vasishtha	Surya
10.	7.63.1-5	Vasishtha	Surya
11.	7.66.14-16	Vasishtha	Surya
12.	8.18.9	Irimbidhi Kaandava	Surya, Agni
13.	8.56.5	Medya Kaandava	Surya, Agni, Ashivano
14.	8.101.11,12	Jamdagni Bhaargava	Surya
15.	10.136	Munyo Vaataarshanaa	Surya, Agni, Vayu

More than 400 Rishis have contributed in Rig Veda out of whom only 13, i.e., 3.4% have addressed their Suktas or Mantras to Surya Devata. Some others have also referred to Surya Devata while addressing their Mantras to some other gods. Scholars should try to know the reasons why so few Rishis have addressed their Mantras to such an important Devata as Surya Devata.[1]

A reading of Rig Veda provides the following important information about Surya Devata:

1. Rishi Abhitapa Saurya opines that *Surya Devata is the son of Aakaasha* (10.37.1). The author tried to know

[1]It can be conjectured that if all the Rishis of Rig Veda and their Mantras can be arranged in a chronological order, it will reveal how, gradually, Rishis found out facts about god Surya and why more Rishis did not write more facts about it. Was it because they could not find out more facts?

why the Rishi has called Surya Devata the son of Aakaasha.

17 Rishis of Rig Veda have given their views on Aakaasha. These Rishis have differentiated between *Aakaasha* and *Antariksha.* For example, Rishi Deerghatamaa Auchathya says that Aakaasha is bigger and wider than Antariksha and Antariksha is a part of Aakaasha (1.160.2, 1.164.33). Other Rishis agree (1.90.7).

What the modern science has to say on this point? Let us see.

Science tells us that the distance between the sun and our earth is 9.3 crore miles. It further reveals that upto 300 miles above the earth, we find air and also the gravitation force of earth. Beyond this 300 miles, there is vacuum and the solar system starts.

When Rishis called Surya Devata the son of Aakaasha, probably they were describing the location of the Surya Devata. By differentiating between Aakaasha and Antariksha, they conveyed the idea that Antariksha is limited to the zone upto which earth's gravitation force works and there is air. Beyond this, is Aakaasha which is the area of operation of Surya Devata.

This view gets confirmed when Rishi Praskadva Kaandava says that Surya Devata has his own solar system in which he shines (8.56.5). Rishi Vasishtha confirms it (7.66.16). Rishi Vibrahaat Saurya says that amongst the planets of the solar system Surya Devata has the best of light, the most excellent (10.170.3).

Rishi Madhuchandaa Vaishvaamitra says that Indra[2] elevated the Surya Devata (in Aakaasha) so that all things can become visible (1.7.3). Other Rishis indirectly confirm it (10.120.1). Rishi Praskadva Kaandava says that the Surya traverses the vast ethereal space (1.50.5, 7). It can, therefore, be said that it was not a very correct statement but only an effort to raise Indra to godhood.

All this goes to show that Rishis have called Surya Devata the son of Aakaasha because he has his own independent solar system and he traverses the Aakaasha, keeping away from Antariksha. But it cannot be said definitely that the god Aakaasha has no other relation with god Surya.

It is strange that what the Rishis of Rig Veda have said a few thousand years ago, the modern science is finding the same today. This confirms the hypothesis that Surya Devata and the Sun are one and the same.

2. Another Rishi, Agastya, gives another view. He says that Surya Devata is the *son of Mother Aditi*. So, Surya is called an Aaditya.

   The natural question that arises is: Who is mother Aditi? And how is she the mother of Surya Devata?

---

[2]The author, in another study on Indra Devata, discovered that initially Rig Veda describes Indra as a human being, a leader of five tribes and wedded to social well-being of people. Probably, as per *Karma* Theory (Action Theory) he was raised to godhood and a search started to give him a suitable place. First, Indra was equated to Surya Devata, then he was made the creator of Surya. Thereafter, he was made the red rays of Surya, the green rays of Surya and ultimately fixed as the god of rainfall.

3. Several Rishis opine that *Surya Devata is illuminating* (1.7.3, 1.50.1, 4, 5; 10.120.1). Rishis Praskadva Kaandava says that Surya Devata, because of his illumination, separates night with day (1.50.7). In other words, Surya Devata is the giver of light and creator of day.

   Rishi Agastya reveals that Surya Devata rises in the east (1.191.8). He further says that Surya rises and verily all beings animated by Surya proceed and execute their assigned labours (7.63.4).

   The question arises: From where Surya Devata gets light? He is son of Mata Aditi. Does he get this light from her? If yes, how?

4. Rishi Vasishtha gives another character of Surya Devata. He reveals that *Surya Devata scorches the regions* (7.34.19). In other words, he has the heat. It is worth knowing from where Surya Devata gets heat? Does he inherit this also, like light, from mother Aditi.

   All this forces us to try to know about mother Aditi.

   Surya Devata is the son of Mother Aditi and so he is an Aaditya (1.191.9). Rishis reveal that mother Aditi has also other sons, i.e., Aadityaas such as Mitra, Savita, Bhaga, Aryaman, Daksha, Ansha, Varuna, Indra, etc. There is no unanimity on their number. Some say they are six (2.27.1), some say seven (9.114.3), some ten and some say twelve (7.51.3).

   A reading of these Aadityaas shows that all of them have the properties akin to Surya Devata—light and heat. The readings of Mantras on mother Aditi reveal that she is a source of celestial light (4.25.3,

10.36.3). The songs about her permanent light are sung (7.82.10[3]). A Rishi has called illuminating Usha as the face of mother Aditi (1.113.19).

The material found in Rig Veda could not help the author to identify mother Aditi. So, he turned to modern Science for the clue. Our hypothesis that Surya Devata of Rig Veda and the Sun are identical leads us to study this angle. The science reveals the following facts about the Sun:

1. The sun is about 9.3 crore miles away from the earth.
2. Sun, in shape, is like a ball.
3. Sun has two parts:
   a. *Central Part* known as core part or Photosphere. Science tells us that continuous nuclear fusion is taking place in this part with the result that its temperature is very high—2×10^7 K. This is the source of heat and light of the Sun. It has also a lot of gases of different types.
   b. *Outer Part* or Chromosphere. This is also hot due to inner part. It has also a lot of gases.

Science tells us that the Energy Rays, which have heat and light, start from the central part of the Sun and move all around. They also reach the earth in different bands of wavelengths. This information was a clear indication that the Sun gets its heat and light from this central part and so, in terms of Rishis of Rig Veda, it should be mother Aditi.

---

[3]Vide A.A. Macdonell, Vedic Mythology, Varanasi, 1984, p. 232.

This view got more confirmed by Mantra 10.189.2 which reveals that the light and heat of Surya Devata comes from the centre of the Surya Devata itself which science calls Photosphere, where nuclear fusion is taking place.

This scientific description helped in identifying not only mother Aditi but several others—Surya Sarpa Ragyi, Dadhikra, Ashivano, Suryaa, seven colour rays and god Varuna (The lord of all waters).

Thus, our hypothesis has been proved correct. Surya Devata of Rig Veda and the Sun of today are one and the same.

Since Surya Devata gets heat and light from his own central part, which Rishis call Mata Aditi, he becomes an Aaditya, a child of mother Aditi, but then, he is a child in a different sense than the other Aadityas.

ADVANTAGES FROM SURYA DEVATA

Vedic Rishis have spelled the following advantages of Surya Devata:

1. Surya Devata, by spreading light and heat, ends the night. The day starts. He is the creator of the day.

2. Bright and glorious Surya Devata rises and diffuses light; verily all beings animated by Surya proceed and execute their assigned labours (7.63.4). Thus, he makes people to start their day's activities.

3. Rishi Abhitapa Saurya reveals that Surya, by dispensing darkness and with his radiance, removes from us famine, sickness and evil dreams (10.37.4). Today, modern science seems to agree. Not only this. The Sun is said to be an alternative source of energy,

called solar energy, and today its various rays are used for treatments of various ills. Ultra red rays is one example. The Rishis reveal that the green rays of Surya Devata are beneficial for vegetation, animals, specially cows and maintenance of ecological balances. Science has to study this aspect.

To sum up, Surya Devata of Rig Veda and the Sun of today are one and the same. It is, as Rishis rightly said, a great god, giver of heat and light, causes rainfall and remover of famines and sickness.

Chapter 2

Mata Aditi and Mausi Diti

Mata Aditi is famous as the mother of Aadityaas. In most of the referenes concerning her she is associated with one or the other Aaditya. A.A. Macdonell opines that in Rig Veda her name has been referred to eighty times. But in spite of this only one Rishi, Satyadhritirvaaruni offers only one full Sukta to mother Aditi (10.184).

Rishi Kutsa Aangirasa and Rishi Gratsamada have offered only one Mantra each, viz., 1.94.16 and 2.40.6 respectively to Mata Aditi.

Scholars say that the word Aditi is from the root *Da* which means "*to bind*". Aditi, therefore, means "*to loosen*" or "*to free*". The question arises: Whom Mother Aditi frees or loosens. Probably both Indian and foreign scholars have missed the hint and have not tried to study Mata Aditi from this angle.

The children of Mata Aditi, behind her name, are called Aadityaas. Surya is an Aaditya. The names of other Aadityaas have been given at several places. Some Aadityaas are—Surya, Mitra, Usha, Savita, Bhaga, Varuna, Indra, Aryaman, Daksha and Ansha.

In Rig Veda only names of Aryaman, Daksha and Ansha have been mentioned at several places such as in Mantras 8.18.3 and 2.27.1. Rishis have not described them or given their characteristics. So, it is difficult to identify them even with the help of modern science. Scholars should find out why Rishis have done so. On the other hand, we find any number of Mantras on Surya, Mitra, Varuna and Indra. Does the difference, indirectly, is related with their respective importance? Probably not. Then a question arises: How Surya, Varuna and Indra are the sons of Mother Aditi? My reading of Rig Veda shows that probably they are not children of Mother Aditi in the same sense as other Aadityaas are. This view needs an indepth study.

In Rig Veda there is no unanimity about the number of Aadityaas. At one place, their number is six (2.27.1), at another seven (9.114.3) and at other place it goes upto twelve (7.56.3). It is worthwhile to know why Rishis are not unanimous about their number. Has it something to do with the new discoveries made by Rishis with time, or that Surya, Varuna and Indra fall in a separate category than the rest, but they were also considered Aaditya proper or both.

A study of Rig Veda provides the following characteristics of Mother Aditi:

1. As the name indicates, *Mata Aditi is a mother.* She is a mother of six or seven or ten or twelve Aadityaas. The

writer feels that wise Rishis, by describing Aditi as mother, wanted to convey the idea that almost all Aadityaas have the same characteristics as Mother Aditi. The proverb is that children are born with some characteristics of mother and father. It is clear that both Indian and foreign scholars missed this implied hint and so could not identify Mother Aditi and Aadityaas.

2. Mother Aditi has *the powers to free people from the physical pains and enable them not to commit moral sins.*[1] She has the powers to expiate the sins (7.93.7). She can exempt disciples from wickedness (1.162.22). By observing the rules of the sons of Aditi, disciples are freed from sins such as in case of Varuna (7.87.7). Mother Aditi, in this sense, is more powerful than other gods. Other gods can, at best, not punish or take note of offences committed against them (Savita, 5.54.3, Prithvi, 10.35.3). But Mother Aditi has the powers by which they cease to commit sins.

   Scholars have not tried to take note of this. They have not tried to know which are the norms or rules of Mother Aditi and by observing their norms or rules, how the idea of not committing sins and leading a pure life comes. However, now scientists have admitted the powers of Mother Aditi and her children to cure several physical ailments. We will discuss it later.

3. *Mother Aditi is Light Giver.* Prayers are offered to her for celestial light (10.36.3, 4.25.3) and also that the light of Aditi be innoxious to us (7.82.10).

[1]A.A. Macdonell, Vedic Mythology, Varanasi, 1984, p. 232.

Illuminating Usha is compared with the face of the Mother Aditi (1.113.19).

4. Max Muller, A.A. Macdonell and others say that Mother *Aditi is infinite.* She is limitless. In this sense she is compared with the sky. Both opine that Aditi is both limitless and immortal. It is worth investigating how Mother Aditi is omnipresent, omnipotent, limitless and immortal.

The above mentioned properties of Mother Aditi forced the writer to try to identify her, to try to know why has she been called mother of Aadityaas? Who are these Aadityaas? What are the norms or rules of Mother Aditi and her Aadityaas, etc.? This led to the study of different Aadityaas. To make the study more fruitful, efforts were made to take the help of modern science. This, of course, removed the curtain and the truth appeared like Sun in the sky.

SURYA DEVATA

Surya Devata is called an Aaditya, son of Mother Aditi, though according to author (as has been shown later), he is slightly different from other Aadityaas. Rishis of Rig Veda give the following information about Surya Devata (as discussed earlier):

1. Rishi Agastya informs that Surya Devata is the son of Mother Aditi (1.191.9).
2. Rishi Praskadva Kaandava opines that Surya Devata has a radiant solar system (8.56.5). Rishi Vasishtha confirms it when he says that illuminating Surya

System appears (7.66.16). Rishi Vibrahaat Saurya says that all illuminating, radiant, mighty Surya displays his vast powers (10.170.2, 3).

3. Surya Devata is illuminating and radiant (1.7.3; 1.50.1, 4, 5; 10.120.1). The natural question that needs answer is why is he illuminating?

4. Rishi Vasishtha states that *Surya scorches the regions* (7.34.19), i.e., he has heat. One should know the source of this heat.

5. *Surya Devata travels in Aakaasha* (1.50.5). *He is lord of seven steeds* (5.45.9). It is worth knowing who are these seven steeds? And what is Aakaasha and how it differs from Antariksha?

The above description gave an impression to the writer that Rishis of Rig Veda are conveying that Surya Devata is a natural phenomenon, who has its own solar system, who travels in Aakaasha, who is giver of light and heat, who is lord of seven steeds, who has set rules and norms and who is son of Mother Aditi and so is also an Aaditya. This information led the author to two conclusions, viz.

a. Mother Aditi must also be a natural phenomenon and also giver of light and heat.

b. Surya Devata and Sun, which we see daily, must be one and the same. This hypothesis needs further confirmation.

So, the writer took the help of science to know about the Sun. Science provided the following facts:

a. Our Sun is like a ball which has two parts:

1. *Core Part* (or Inner Part)—This part is also a small ball, which is located at the centre of the Sun. The temperature of this part is very high—2×10^7 K to be precise. Science tells us that in this part there are various gases like Oxygen, Hydrogen and also particles of various metals such as Iron, Sodium, Calcium, etc. Continuous Nuclear Fusion is taking place in this core part of the Sun, between these metals etc. which causes tremendous temperature. Naturally, this generates heat and light, travels all around, away from the core of the Sun. This part is known as Photosphere.

2. *Outer Part*—This outer part is also like a bigger ball. Inside this ball is the small ball of the core part. Due to the heat and light of the core part, this part has also heat and light and lot of gases

SUN

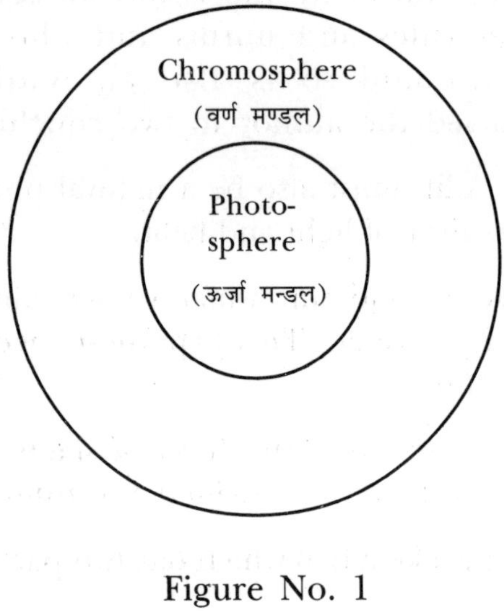

Figure No. 1

but its temperature is lesser than the inner part. This part is known as Chromosphere.

Sun and its both parts can be shown through Figure No. 1.

b. The energy generated by the collusion of various particles is not the same. It varies from particle to particle.

c. The energy created by the Nuclear Fusion in the Core Part of the Sun travels in waves all around and reaches the earth also in various *Bands.*

d. These energy waves travel with the help of energy particles. One particle passes the energy to another and so the onward motion continues. These energy particles are called *Photons.*

e. The energy particles do not move in a straight line. They move onward in a roundabout way. Figure No. 2 demonstrates it.

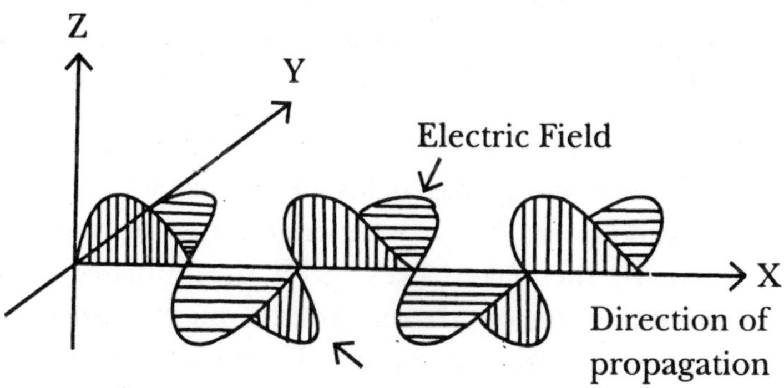

Figure No. 2

f. The energy of a particle and its wavelength are inversely related. This relationship is demonstrated by Figure No. 3.

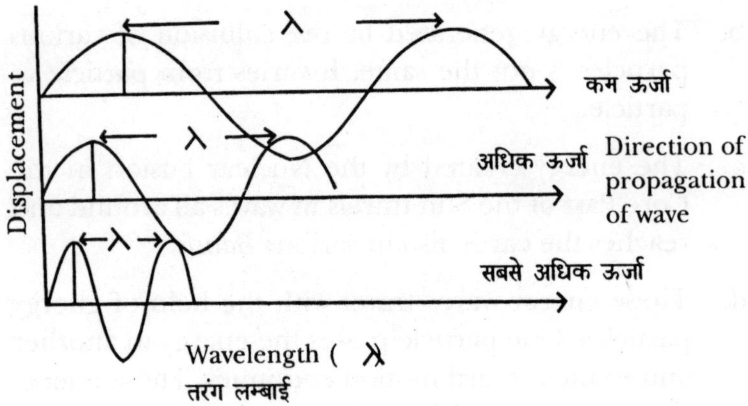

Figure No. 3

g. Science tells us that the energy waves reach earth in three bands, viz.

1. *Band One*—It consists of the energy waves which have the highest energy particles, i.e., where wavelengths are shortest. These wavelengths cannot be seen on earth by naked eyes.

2. *Band Two*—It consists of the energy waves which have lower energy particles, i.e., whose wavelengths are moderate. These wavelengths can be seen on earth by the naked eyes. After the Sunrise, these moderate wavelengths reach earth, one after another, and are of different colours. Their colours are Red, Orange, Yellow, Green, Blue, Indigo and Violet.

3. *Band Three*—It consists of the energy waves which have the lowest energy particles but longest wave-

lengths. These wavelengths also cannot be seen on earth by the naked eyes.

A comparison of this scientific knowledge about the Sun with the views expressed by Rishis of Rig Veda about Surya Devata revealed several similarities to the author, viz.

1. That the inner or core part of the Sun, called Photosphere, where due to Nuclear Fusion, high temperature is generated and the various energy waves travel all around and reach earth also in three bands, should be, in terms of Vedic Rishis, Mother Aditi. There are many similarities in their characteristics.

2. That the outer part of the Sun, called Chromosphere, should be Aunt Diti. The proximity of the Inner Part and the Outer Part and some common characteristics show it.

3. That what we call Nuclear Fusion in science should be *Surya Sarparagyi* in Vedic Rishis' language.

   We find only one Sukta (10.189) in Rig Veda on *Surya Sarparagyi* which has been given by a Rishi whose name is Saarpi Raagyo. Mantra (10.189.2) reveals that the radiance which emits from the Surya comes from its centre. The scientific veiw and the view of Rishis seems to be identical.

4. The energy waves, according to science, travel with the help of Photons—the energy particles. And these Photons do not travel in a straight line. They move onward in a roundabout way. Rishis, it appears, call Photons *Dadhikra Deva*. Rishi Vaamdeva opines that

Dadhikra is swift (4.39.1), those who are preparing for battle invoke *Dadhikra* who has been compared with a horse (4.39.5), *Dadhikra* is a rapid steed (4.39.6). Aditi renders him free from sin who has performed the worship of the steed *Dadhikra* at the time when the fire has been kindled at the opening of the dawn (4.39.3). Vaamdeva further reveals that horse accelerates his paces. *Dadhikra* following the winding of the roads, goes still more rapidly (4.40.4). Rishi Vasishtha confirms it when he says "*Dadhikravan*, the swift steed, the first (horses), knowing (his office), is in the front of the chariots (of the gods), consentient with Ushas, with Surya, with the Aadityaas, with the Vasus..." (7.44.4).

A.A. Macdonell, while discussing the origin of the word *Dadhikra,* says that it means spreading *Dadhi* at the time of the Sunrise.[2]

5. That the two bands of energy waves, i.e., the shortest and the longest energy waves, which cannot be seen by the naked eyes on earth, in the words of Rishis of Rig Veda, are two handsome young gods called Ashvins.

   Some foreign scholars or even Indian scholars have misinterpreted the word Ashvino. For example Max Muller, Griffith, Wilson, etc. interpret it to mean two horses. It conveys no sense when seen with reference to the context. Some Indian scholars associate them with scholars like *Dasrau, Naasatyo, Ashivano* and some other scholars with three *Gunas—Satoguna, Rajoguna* and *Tapoguna.* Arya Muni opines that

[2]A.A. Macdonell, op. cit., p. 283.

Ashvino is from the root Ashu which means the power which is quickly absorbed.[3]

The reading of Rig Veda reveals that Ashvino is ever youthful (7.67.10), they are invested with solar radiance (8.8.2), they have fascinating complexion (8.26.6), are illustrious (7.68.1), they ride a golden chariot (5.75.3) and Usha awake the Ashvino (8.9.17). All this and association with chariot, horses, etc. which are indicator of the speed, leaves little doubt that two energy wave bands of science and Ashvino of Rig Veda are one and the same.

This conclusion is further confirmed when Rishi Vishwaamitra informs "the parent of twins (the dawn), has brought both the twin (Ashvino) on this occasion, ...the dispersers of darkness, assuming bodies as a pair (of twins) at the origin of the day" (3.39.3). Ashvino have been married with Suryaa, the daughter of Surya Devata and the bridal procession has been despatched by *Savita Devata* (10.85.13) and gods *Bhaga*, *Aryaman*, *Savita*, etc. have given *Suryaa* to *Ashvino* (10.85.36). Thus, Surya Deva and his different energy waves of different colours are connected with Ashvino.

6. Science says that there are three bands of energy waves. In between the bands of energy waves which have the longest wavelength and the shortest wavelength, is the third band of moderate wavelength which can be seen on earth by naked eyes. This third band has seven colour energy rays.

---

[3]Arya Muni, Rig Veda Bhashya, Mudrit George Press, Banaras, 1974, pp. 462-465.

Rishis of Rig Veda talk of the daughter of Surya Deva, called *Suryaa*, who is married to two Ashvino. These two Ashvino are two extreme bands of energy rays. (More about them later.) So, the Rishis, in a poetic way, describe the third middle band as *Suryaa* (daughter of Surya Deva) and say she has been married with the other two bands, Ashvino. Sukta 10.85 describes the marriage of *Suryaa* with the Ashvino. The different colour rays of Surya Deva—Savita, Bhaga, Aryaman, etc. who are also called Aadityaas, come to give a send off to *Suryaa*.

Thus, it is clear that the middle band of energy waves is *Suryaa* of Rig Veda. There is lot of similarity between the two.

7. A study of Aadityaas, the children of Mother Aditi, revealed several interesting facts, viz.

a. Mother Aditi has several Aadityaas, the main ones being Surya Devata, Mitra, Usha, Savita, Bhaga, Aryaman, Daksha, Ansha, Varuna and Indra.

b. The reading about these Aadityaas revealed that Surya Devata, Varuna and Indra fall under a different category than the rest of the Aadityaas, viz., Mitra, Usha, Savita, Bhaga, Aryaman, Daksha and Ansha.

c. Mitra Devata is a Red colour energy rays of Surya.

d. Usha is an Orange colour energy rays.

e. Savita is of Golden colour energy rays.

f. Bhaga is of Green colour energy rays.

The author could not find sufficient material in Rig Veda to identify Aryaman, Daksha and Ansha. But since they are also Aadityaas, they must be having the remaining three colours—blue, indigo and violet. Scholars should try to identify their colours.

Thus, it can be concluded that the middle band of energy waves emitting from Sun, i.e., Mother Aditi (Photosphere) and which is composed of seven colour rays, viz., red, orange, yellow, green, blue, indigo and violet is nothing but the seven Aadityaas of Mother Aditi—Mitra, Usha, Savita, Bhaga, Aryaman, Daksha and Ansha.

The above study convinced me that Rishis of Rig Veda, a few thousand years back, were telling, in their own style, the scientific truths about Mother Aditi. This study helped me in identifying a number of gods, who were not identified in scientific terminology earlier and also finding out that they form one group of these gods. These gods are:

	Rig Veda	*Science*
1.	Mata Aditi	Core Part of the Sun called Photosphere
2.	Mausi Diti	Outer Part of the Sun called Chromosphere
3.	Surya Devata	The Sun
4.	Surya Sarparagyi	Nuclear Fusion in Photosphere
5.	Dadhikra	Photon
6.	Ashvino	Two bands of energy waves, one having the longest wavelength and the other shortest wave length

7.	Suryaa	The middle energy band consisting of seven colour rays which is visible by naked eyes on earth
8.	Seven Aadityaas	Seven colour rays of the middle energy band visible on earth

Aaditya-Gan

Chapter 3

Mitra Devata[1]

A.A. Macdonell has rightly said that only one Sukta, i.e., 3.59 has been offered to Mitra Devata by Rishi Vishwaamitra and other Suktas have been offered jointly to Mitra and Varuna.[2] In spite of this observation, A.A. Macdonell or other scholars have not tried to find out the reason for this.

The following Rishis have offered or addressed their Mantras to Mitra Devata:

	Rishi	*Mantra*	*God whom offered*
1.	Vishwaamitra	3.59	Mitra
2.	Vishwaamitro Jamdagni	3.62, 16-18	Mitra, Varuna

[1]Author's study reveals that Mitra Devata is the red colour energy ray coming from the Sun on Earth at dawn time and going away at the time of Sunset.

[2]A.A. Macdonell, Vedic Mythology, Varanasi, 1984, pp. 53-54.

	Rishi	*Mantra*	*God whom offered*
3.	Vasishtha	7.63.2, 7.50.1, 7.60.2-12, 7.6.1, 7.62.4-6, 7.63.5-6, 7.64, 7.65, 7.66, 1-3, 17-19	Mitra, Varuna
4.	Shruta Vidaatreya	5.62	Mitra, Varuna
5.	Archanaanaa Aatreya	5.63, 5.64	Mitra, Varuna
6.	Raata-Havya Aatreya	5.65, 5.66	Mitra, Varuna
7.	Yajata Aatreya	5.67, 5.68	Mitra, Varuna
8.	Uroocha Kriraatreya	5.69, 5.70	Mitra, Varuna
9.	Vaahu-Vrakta Aatreya	5.71, 5.72	Mitra, Varuna
10.	Paruchepau Devodaasi	1.136.1-5, 1.137, 1.139.2	Mitra, Varuna
11.	Medhaatithi Kaandava	1.15.6 1.23.4-6	Mitra, Varuna Mitra, Varuna
12.	Hiranya Stoop Aangirasa	1.35.1	Mitra, Varuna Agni, Raatri, Savita
13.	Kutsa Aangirasa	1.94.16	Mitra, Varuna, Aditi, Sindhu, Prithvi, Dhaunsa, Agni
14.	Kandavo Ghaura	1.43.3	Mitra, Varuna, Rudra
15.	Deerghatamaa Auchathya	1.151.1, 2-9, 1.152, 1.153	Mitra, Varuna
16.	Gratsamada	2.36.6, 2.41.4-6	Mitra, Varuna
17.	Madhuchandaa Vishwaamitra	1.2.7-9	Mitra, Varuna
18.	Bharadwaajo Vaarhaspatya	6.67	Mitra, Varuna
19.	Vishvamanaa Vaivashva	8.25.1-9, 13-14	Mitra, Varuna
20.	Jamdagni Bhaargava	8.101.1-5	Mitra, Varuna
21.	Shakapooto Naarmedha	10.132.2-7	Mitra, Varuna

The above table shows that out of more than 400 Rishis of Rig Veda only 21, i.e., 5%, have offered or addressed their Mantras/Suktas to Mitra Devata and out of these 21, twenty have offered them jointly with Varuna or other Devatas. One should try to assess whether this indicates the relative importance of Mitra Devata. One should also try to arrange these Rishis in a chronological order so that one may be able to know how the thought process has developed.

It is to be noted here that out of 21 Rishis noted above six, i.e., 28.3%, belong to family of Rishi Aatreya. Does it show that family of Rishi Aatreya tried to specialise on the study of Mitra Devata and became an authority on it?

WHO IS MITRA DEVATA

Rishi Yajata Aatreya says that divine *Mitra Devata is an Aaditya*, i.e., child of Mother Aditi (5.67.1). Another Aatreya, Rishi Uroocha Kriraatreya testifies it and adds that Mitra Devata and Varuna Devata were born in the celestial world or solar world (5.69.4). Other Rishis confirm that Mitra Devata is the son of Mother Aditi. Some such Rishis are: Rishi Gratsamada (2.41.6), Rishi Vishwamanaa Vaivashva (8.25.3) and Rishi Shakapooto Naarmedha (10.132.6).

Rishis of Rig Veda clearly and repeatedly state that the children of Mother Aditi are: Surya, Mitra, Savita, Varuna, Indra, Bhaga, Daksha, Aryaman and Ansha. However, after studying Rig Veda along with elementary science, the author has reached the conclusion that though Surya and Varuna are also children of Mother Aditi but they are children in a different sense than the rest.

The author, on the basis of his studies of Rig Veda and modern science, has reached the following conclusions:

i) The core part of the Sun, known as Photosphere, where continuous nuclear fusion is taking place, is nothing else but Mother Aditi in terms of Rishis (explained earlier).

ii) Surya Devata or Sun gets the heat and light from core part, i.e., Mother Aditi. Hence, he is the son of Aditi. But since Aditi is a part of Surya Devata, he is a son in a different sense than the other Aadityaas like Mitra, Savita, Bagha, Daksha, Aryaman and Ansha.

iii) Varuna Devata, as per Rishis, is the lord of waters—oceans, waters below the earth and waters above the earth. Science tells us that long long back a part of the young Sun broke. This broken part was also very hot, full with metal particles and gases. This was our earth. With time, it started cooling down. So metal particles started concentrating at the central or core part of our earth and hence, from this part the gases were pushed out. The mixture of a few gases of the earth formed ocean and waters below the earth. Thus, Varuna Devata was born. Obviously, he is also the son of Mother Aditi but in a different sense.

iv) Other Aadityaas—Mitra, Usha, Savita, Bagha, Daksha, Aryaman and Ansha are energy waves of different colours which are also released by Mother Aditi and can be seen with the naked eyes on earth.

In order to verify the above conclusion of the author, viz., Mitra Devata is an energy wave released by Mother Aditi, which has a colour and which can be seen on earth, let us turn to what Rishis say on the topic.

Rishi Vasishtha associates Mitra Devata with Surya Devata. He reveals that Mitra Devata spreads beautiful light before the rise of Surya (7.61.1) and calls Surya Devata the eye of Mitra (7.63.1). He further reveals that Mitra is one of the seven steeds of Surya Devata (7.60.3). Rishis worship Mitra when the Surya has risen (7.63.5). They invoke Mitra when the Surya has risen (7.65.1, 7.66.7). Mitra animates men to exertion (7.36.2).

All the above mentioned facts given by Rishis show a close relationship between the Surya Devata and Mitra. For example, Mitra arrives on earth prior to Surya Devata and that Mitra is one of the seven steeds of Surya Devata.

Science tells that a band of seven colour rays, which have moderate wavelengths, and can be seen by naked eyes on earth, arrive on earth at the time of Sunrise in a given order. The first to come is Red colour energy wave followed by Orange, Yellow, Green, Blue, Indigo and Violet colour energy rays. So, by comparing the views of Rishis on Mitra Devata with science, one reaches the conclusion that Mitra Devata should be Red colour rays emitting from Mother Aditi as Rishis have described Usha Devi having orange colour.

This conclusion is confirmed by Rishi Archanaanaa Aatreya when he says that Mitra Devata causes the purple (read red) and faultless sky to send down rain (5.63.6).

A PROBLEM

Rishis of Rig Veda describe Indra as the son of Mother Aditi. He is equated with Surya Devata (8.89.1, 2, 1.100.6, 1.103.1) and shown as illuminator of earth (3.44.4). He is also depicted riding a chariot driven by red colour horses (1.6.2, 4.32.24). This gives the impression that Indra may be red colour ray emitted by Mother Aditi. If so, how can then Mitra be red colour ray? It becomes a problem.

A close reading of Rig Veda shows that Rishis of Rig Veda are not unanimous about Indra. There are Rishis who show Indra with a green nose (6.29.5, 6), green moustaches and green beard (10.105.7) and riding a chariot driven by green coloured horses (3.30.23, 3.31.3). Obviously, Indra cannot be both a red ray and a green ray.

Rishis, ultimately, fix Indra as a god of rainfall.

So, it appears that Rishis were making experiments to know actually who Indra is. So, in this search they thought he may be a red colour ray of Mata Aditi but later they themselves rejected this idea.

ANOTHER PROBLEM

In Rig Veda most of the Rishis opine that Mitra and Varuna are children of Mother Aditi and they are very close to each other and so most of the Suktas or Mantras have been offered jointly to them. The riddle is that a reading of Rig Veda makes it clear that Mitra is the red colour ray of the Mother Aditi and Varuna is the god of waters. If so, what could be the connection between Mitra and Varuna?

The riddle becomes more complex when Rishis say that Mitra contributes in the rainfall (5.62.3, 5.63.1.4, 5.67.4, 5.68.2, 5.69.2, 7.64.1, 7.66.9). One fails to find out the relationship between the red colour ray of the Sun and its capacity to cause rainfall. One will have to take the help of science.

Science tells us that Infra-Red Rays, which are not visible on earth, are hottest. After Infra-Red Rays come Red Rays. Red Rays are the hottest amongst the seven colour rays, that are visible on earth and are also responsible for creating heat effect similar to that of Infra-Red Rays. So, Red Rays, i.e., god Mitra causes greatest evaporation of water amongst the seven colour rays of the Sun. Thus, god Mitra's contribution in formation of clouds and consequent rainfall is maximum. The Rishis of Rig Veda could know this scientific fact and so they offer their Mantras jointly to Mitra and Varuna.

ADVANTAGES FROM MITRA DEVATA

Rishis opine that Mitra Devata bestows several advantages on man, viz.

1. Red colour rays help in rainfall and consequently vegetation is good and more corn is grown.

   The author could not establish any relationship between the rainfall and Mitra Devata.

2. Due to rainfall cows become healthier and their yield increases.

3. When Mitra appears on the sky, beautiful light is spread on the earth. This is an end of the night. It animates man, animals and birds to exertion. Production activities start.

4. Author feels that red colour rays are a cure to several diseases. Today orthopaedic doctors give red colour radiation to the patients with muscular or bone ailments. Rishis of Rig Veda have not directly mentioned this advantage but later Rishis have narrated this advantage at length.

Chapter 4

Usha Devi

Mata Aditi is the mother of Aadityaas. All of them, like her, are light giver, illuminator and scorcher. But the Rishis are not unanimous about their number and names. For example, Surya Devata is called an Aaditya by some (1.191.9) but others do not call him an Aaditya. In Mantra 2.27.1, the names of six Aadityaas—Mitra, Bhaga, Aryaman, Daksha, Ansha and Varuna have been given but in this list Surya Devata does not find a place. Again, some Rishis opine that there are seven Aadityaas (9.114.3), some say ten and yet others opine that they are twelve (7.51.3). Probably, this is because of gradual discoveries taking place in a period of time. Again, Usha Devi has not been called an Aaditya directly, probably because she is a goddess. It is unfortunate that till this date the scholars have not tried to arrange the Rishis of Rig Veda in a chronological order which would have given a clear idea of the development of ideas on a subject.

A reading of Rig Veda gives the impression that Usha Devi is not an Aaditya. But this is not a correct conclusion. Rishis after Rishis have called Bhaga Devata an Aaditya. Interestingly, Rishi Deerghatamaa Auchathya calls Usha Devi a sister of Bhaga Aaditya (1.123.5). Obviously, this means that Usha Devi should also be an Aaditya. This is confirmed by a reading of other Rishis on the subject.

We find the following Suktas and Mantras in Rig Veda on Usha Devi:

	Sukta	*Rishi*	*God*
1.	1.48	Praskadva Kaandava	Usha
2.	1.49	Praskadva Kaandava	Usha
3.	1.123	Kakshivaan Dairdhtamasa (Aushija)	Usha
4.	1.124	Kakshivaan Dairdhtamasa (Aushija)	Usha
5.	3.61	Vishwaamitra	Usha
6.	4.51	Vaamdeva	Usha
7.	4.52	Vaamdeva	Usha
8.	5.79	Satyashravaa Aatreya	Usha
9.	5.80	Satyashravaa Aatreya	Usha
10.	6.64	Bharadwaajo Vaarhaspatya	Usha
11.	6.65	Bharadwaajo Vaarhaspatya	Usha
12.	7.75	Vasishtha	Usha
13.	7.76	Vasishtha	Usha
14.	7.77	Vasishtha	Usha
15.	7.78	Vasishtha	Usha
16.	7.79	Vasishtha	Usha
17.	7.80	Vasishtha	Usha
18.	7.81	Vasishtha	Usha
19.	10.172	Samvarta	Usha

	Mantra	*Rishi*	*God*
1.	1.30.20.2	Shuneha Shepa Aajeegarti	Usha
2.	1.92.1-15	Gautama Raahugana	Usha
3.	1.113.1-20	Kutsa Aangirasa	Usha
4.	3.55.1	Prajaapati Vaishwaamitra, Prajaapati Vaachya	Usha
5.	7.41.7	Vasishtha	Usha
6.	1.44.1, 2	Praskadva Kaandava	Usha, Agni, Ashvino
7.	1.113.1	Kutsa Aangirasa	Usha, Raatri
8.	4.30.9-11	Vaamdeva	Usha, Indra
9.	8.47.14-18	Trita Aaptya	Usha, Aaditya
10.	8.101.13	Jamdagni Bhaargava	Usha, Surya, Prabha

Out of more than 400 Rishis of Rig Veda only 16 Rishis, i.e., 3.93% Rishis have offered their Suktas or Mantras to Usha. It is worth enquiring why so few Rishis have studied Usha Devi.

The above list of Rishis, who have offered their Suktas or Mantras to Usha Devi, shows that Rishi Vasishtha has offered the maximum number of Suktas and Mantras to Usha Devi. It appears he has tried to specialise on her.

A study of the material on Usha Devi gives the following information:

WHO IS USHA DEVI?

a) Rishi Praskadva Kaandava says that Usha Devi is the daughter of heaven, i.e., Aakaasha (1.48.1, 8, 9). Rishi Kakshivaana Dairdhtamasa (Aushija) agrees (1.124.3). Rishi Vasishtha (7.81.1), Rishi Shuneha Shepa Aajeegarti (1.30.20), Rishi Gautama Raahugana

(1.92.5) and Rishi Kutsa Aangirasa (1.113.7) confirm this view.

It is necessary to know why these Rishis are saying that Usha Devi is the daughter of Aakaasha or heaven? The studies of Aakaasha in Rig Veda reveal that Rishis differentiated between Aakaasha and Antariksha but consider Aakaasha and heaven synonym. They reveal that Aakaasha is wider and bigger than Antariksha (who, at best, is a part of it) and in reality Aakaasha is beyond Antariksha though it includes Antariksha also.

Science seems to confirm this view. Science tells that upto 300 miles away towards the Sun, there is air and gravitation force of earth. Beyond this, there is vacuum. Science also tells that the distance between the Sun and the earth is 9.3 crore miles. So, Antariksha seems to be upto 300 miles from the earth where there is air and earth's gravitation. Beyond this, in vacuum, is heaven or Aakaasha whose area is spread in a radius of 9.29 crore miles. Normally, this makes Aakaasha limitless, wide etc.

Rishis opine that the Surya Devata travels in Aakaasha, i.e., beyond Antariksha.

From this it can be inferred that like Surya Devata, Usha Devi also travels in Aakaasha. This naturally establishes a close proximity between the two and so Rishis call her the daughter of Aakaasha.

b) Rishi Vasishtha says that Usha Devi is the daughter of heaven (7.78.4, 7.79.3). These Rishis have also called Usha the daughter of Aakaasha. Rishis nowhere differentiate between Aakaasha and heaven. So, it can be presumed that Rishis, presuming Aakaasha and heaven synonym, called Usha the daughter of heaven also.

c) Rishi Kakshivaana Dairdhtamasa (Aushija) opines that Usha Devi is the sister of Varuna and Bhaga (1.123.5). Rishis tell that both Varuna and Bhaga are the children of Mata Aditi. So, it appears, these Rishis, indirectly, are saying that Usha Devi is also a child of Mother Aditi.

   Science accepts a close relationship between Mata Aditi (Photosphere) and Usha Devi (a ray of the middle band of rays) and also accepts a relationship between Varuna (God of Rainfall) and Mata Aditi.

   Rishis also call Usha the daughter of Aakaasha. This also gives weight to the above conclusion that Usha is the daughter of Mata Aditi.[1]

d) Rishi Vaamdeva calls Usha the daughter of Surya (the Sun) (4.51.1, 10,11). Rishi Satya Shravaa Aatreya (5.79, 2, 3, 8, 9, 5.80.5, 6) and Rishi Trita Aaptya (8.47.14) confirm it. According to this statement of Rishis, Usha should be the granddaughter of Mother Aditi as Surya himself is the son of Mata Aditi. This also establishes a relationship between Mata Aditi and Usha but it is worth investigating why a Rishi of the eminence of Vaamdeva has called Usha the daughter of Surya, i.e., granddaughter of Mata Aditi.

---

[1]Science tells that the core part of the Sun, due to nuclear fusion, is very hot and full of gases. The mix of some of these gases—Oxygen and Hydrogen, etc. creates water. Rishis call it Varuna Devata.

e) Rishi Vishwaamitra reveals that Usha is the wife of Surya Devata (3.61.4). One Rishi says that Usha is the daughter of Surya and the other Rishi opines that she is the wife of Surya. Both statements cannot be correct. It simply shows that the Rishis were exploring and they had not reached a definite conclusion by that time. But then certainly it shows that the Rishis felt that there is a proximity of Surya Devata and Usha.[2]

f) As per interpretation of H.H. Wilson, Rishi Kutsa Aangirasa calls Usha illuminator and a rival of Mother Aditi (1.113.19). This does not go down well with logic as other Rishis have called Usha the daughter of Surya, wife of Surya and sister of Varuna and Bhaga. All this shows that Usha has a close relationship with Mother Aditi. How can then she be her rival?

Another scholar has interpreted this Mantra to mean that Usha is the face of Mother Aditi, who appears early in the morning and illuminates the sacrificer. This seems to be more correct.

The above narration clearly shows that Usha has a close relationship with Mother Aditi and her other children. Like Aadityaas, she is also illuminator and she appears early in the morning.

When we examine the above facts with the help of science, it immediately becomes clear that Usha is one of the Rays of the middle Band coming from Mother Aditi on earth and should be of Orange colour.

---

[2]If we can arrange the ideas of Rishis in a chronological order, it will iron out these differences and show how the ideas have grown on the basis of new researches.

CHARACTERISTICS OF USHA

1. Rishi Gautama Raahugana says that Usha and night are sisters, one illuminating the boundaries of the sky and the other (Night) retiring (1.92.11). Rishi Kakshivaana Dairdhtamasa (Aushija) confirms it (1.124.8). Rishi Samvarta elaborates the relationship by saying that Usha is the elder sister of night (10.172.1). Rishi Kutsa Aangirasa says that both Usha and Night are sisters but they are of different colours. They travel the same path alternatively (1.113.3).

   The only interpretation of the above can be that Usha and Night rotate in a circle. The science confirms it and adds that it is because the earth rotates round the Sun.

   Rishi Vasishtha gives a different statement. He says that Usha and Night are not sisters but rivals or enemies to each other. Usha annihilates the darkness (7.79.2). Similar views are expressed in other Mantras (7.75.1, 7.76.7, 7.79.7, 7.81.4). Other Rishis also confirm it (1.92.5, 3.61.4, 4.51.3, 5.80.5, 6.65.1, 6, 10.172.1).

   The author has failed to reconcile these two contradictory statements. A clue has been given by Rishis Kutsa Aangirasa when he says that both (Usha and Night) are allied to the same Sun (1.113.2). Science also says that day and night are formed because of the rotation of earth round the Sun.

2. Rishi Praskadva Kaandava says that Usha is illuminating who illuminates the whole world (1.48.8, 1.49.4). Several Rishis confirm this view such as Rishi Vaamdeva (4.51.1.5, 6, 7.75.1, 7.77.3, 7.80.1), Rishi

Bharadwaajo Vaarhaspatya (6.64.2) and Rishi Gautama Raahugana (1.92.1).

Rishi Praskadva Kaandava says that Usha has bright Rays (1.48.13). Rishi Satya Shravaa Aatreya (5.79.1) and Rishi Shuneha Shepa Aajeegarti (1.30.2, 10) confirm it. Rishi Praskadva Kaandava further adds that she has white complexion (1.49.3). Rishi Vaamdeva (4.51.2) and Rishi Bharadwaajo Vaarhaspatya (6.64.1) confirm it.

Rishi Kakshivaana Dairdhtamasa (Aushija) reveals that Usha is arrayed in light (1.124.3). Rishi Satya Shravaa Aatreya confirms it by saying that she is lustrous and radiant (5.79.4, 10).

Rishi Kutsa Aangirasa opines that Usha is "most excellent luminary of all luminaries" (1.113.1). She gives white shining dawn (1.113.2).

Thus, Rishis say that Usha is illuminating. She has bright Rays, white complexion, she is arrayed in light and she is most excellent luminary of all luminaries. All these adjectives are almost synonyms. But the important question is: From where Usha gets these qualities. Rishis of Rig Veda do not give a direct answer but they give broad hints by associating Usha with Surya, Bhaga, Varuna etc. The author, on the basis of the scientific knowledge, feels that in the core part of the Sun, called Photosphere (whom Rishis call Mata Aditi), continuous nuclear fusion is taking place and various rays are being emitted (from Mata Aditi). One of these rays is Usha Ray which belongs to the middle band of Energy Rays. This middle Band of Energy waves consists of seven colour Rays and can be seen on earth by the naked eyes. That makes Usha a daughter or a sister of Surya and a sister of Bhaga.

3. Rishi Kakshivaana Dairdhtamasa (Aushija) informs that Usha approaches from the east (1.124.11). This statement is confirmed by other Rishis (4.51.1, 2, 7, 5.80.4, 7.76.2).

   Rishi Gautama Raahugana reveals that Usha having lighted up the whole world spreads towards the west (1.92.9). Other Rishis confirm it (1.124.7, 5.80.6).

   A reading of this fact goes to show that Usha, like other Rays and also Surya Devata, rises from east and moves towards west, where she vanishes and her sister, Night, takes over. It is clear that Rishis are revealing a scientific truth.

4. Rishi Vaamdeva opines that Usha is not one single Ray but she has a Band. He tells that it is not possible to distinguish between the first Ray of Usha and the later ones as all of them are alike (4.51.6, 8). Other Rishis agree (1.113.8, 10, 1.124.9, 7.77.5).

   Science accepts that each colour ray does not come single. They come in a Band.

5. Rishi Satya Shravaa Aatreya reveals that Usha appears before the arrival of the Sun (5.80.1). Other Rishis confirm it. Rishi Vasishtha (7.76.3, 7.78.1, 7.80.1), Rishi Vishwaamitra (3.61.7), Rishi Kakshivaana Dairdhtamasa (Aushija) (1.123.9), Rishi Praskadva Kaandava (1.48.7) and Rishi Kutsa Aangirasa (1.113.10) are some of them.

Science says that the first ray to appear on the earth is of Red colour followed by Rays of Orange, Yellow, Green, Blue, Indigo and Violet colour. So, Usha, as the above description reveals, must be the Orange colour Ray.

6. The above view is confirmed by Rishi Bharadwaajo Vaarhaspatya when he says that the chariot of Usha is drawn by purple steeds (6.65.2). Other Rishis agree (3.61.2, 5.80.1, 3, 1.113.14).

   This also confirms the above conclusion.

   This view gets further confirmed by Rishi Shyaavaashva Aatreya when he reveals that the other ray, by the name Savita, shines in sequences to the passage of dawn (5.81.2), Savita Ray is of Yellow colour as explained by Rishis at other places and as per science it comes after Orange colour Ray.

   Rishis say that Usha wakes up birds, animals and men and persuades them to do their functions (1.48.5, 6, 1.113.14, 1.124.4, 4.51.5, 7.75.1, 7.79.1). The activity starts.

   A.A. Macdonell sums up by saying that Usha is the best poetic creation of Vedic period. She comes like a dancer. She wears clothes of light, appears from east and demonstrates her loving beauty.[3]

[3]A.A. Macdonell, Vedic Mythology, Chaukhamba Vidya Bhawan, Varanasi, 1984, p. 87.

Chapter 5

Savita Deva

The following Suktas and Mantras in Rig Veda have been offered or addressed to Savita Deva:

	Sukta	*Rishi*	*God*
1.	2.34	Gratsamada Bhaargava	Savita
2.	4.53	Vaamdeva	Savita
3.	4.54	Vaamdeva	Savita
4.	5.81	Shyaavaashva Aatreya	Savita
5.	5.82	Shyaavaashva Aatreya	Savita
6.	6.71	Bharadwaajo Vaarhaspatya	Savita
7.	7.45	Vasishtha	Savita
8.	10.149	Archan Hiranyastoop	Savita

	Mantra	*Rishi*	*God*
1.	1.22.5, 8	Medhaatithi Kaandava	Savita
2.	1.24.3, 4	Shuneha Shepa Aajeegarti	Savita
3.	1.24.5	Shuneha Shepa Aajeegarti	Savita, Bhaga

4.	1.35, 2-11	Hiranya Stoop Aangirasa	Savita
5.	3.62,10-12	Vishwaamitra	Savita
6.	7.38, 1-5	Vasishtha	Savita
7.	7.38, 6, 7	Vasishtha	Savita
8.	9.67.25, 26	Pavitra, Vasishtha, Bhauma	Savita, Agni
9.	10.139, 1-3	Vishwaavasur Devagandharva	Savita

Other Mantras

1. 1.34.10
2. 1.95.7
3. 1.110.2, 3
4. 1.190.3
5. 2.53.3, 4
6. 3.36.6, 13
7. 3.38.8
8. 3.54.11
9. 4.14.2
10. 4.53.3, 4
11. 7.79.2
12. 10.7.4
10. 34.8

The material on Savita Deva was collected, systematised and then analysed. The results are presented below:

1. *Savita Deva is light* (3.62.10, 4.53.2, 4, 5.81.2) and illuminates others such as Aakaasha (4.53.2), Antariksha (1.35.7, 4.53.5), all regions (4.53.4) and even Vaayu and Prithvi (4.53.3).

   The question arises from where he gets his light and where he gets powers to illuminate others? Rishis do not give direct answer to the question. One will have to infer to get an answer.

2. *Savita with light is also shining* (5.81.3, 5.82.2).

The question arises how is Savita Deva shining? From where he derives this power?

Rishis do not seem to give a direct answer. Again, reliance will have to be made on inferences.

3. *Savita Deva has vast hands. He repeatedly raises them and stretches them* (2.38.2, 4.53.4, 6.71.1). He does it to spread his light and illuminate different regions and thereby purify waters and air (2.38.2, 6.71.1).

   One will like to know the reasons that enable Savita to purify water and air.

4. *Savita Deva is not a single light and illuminating Ray but is a Band of Rays* (5.81.4, 10.139.1). These rays move rapidly (2.38.3).

   All this means that Savita Deva has a Band of Rays which move fast. Why and how is it so? Rishis do not seem to give a direct answer.

5. *Savita Deva illuminates Prithvi in the morning and goes away in the evening.* Rishi Vaamdeva says that Savita Deva "fills (with radiance) the celestial and terrestrial regions and puts forth his arms for (the work of) production, regulating the world and animating it with light" (4.53.3).

   Obviously the Rishi is referring that Savita illuminates Prithvi in the morning. Rishi Shyaavaashva Aatreya confirms it (5.81.1). But he gives several important clues. He reveals that Savita Deva appears after Usha (5.81.2). Then adds, Savita precedes both night and day (5.82.8, 5.81.4). This implies that Savita comes in the morning and leaves in the evening. Rishi Bharadwaajo Vaarhaspatya confirms it (6.71.4).

Science tells us that the seven colour rays of Sun come to earth, one after another, in the morning and they leave in the evening, one after another, in the reverse order. It is certain that Rishis are also saying the same thing about Savita Deva.

6. *Savita Deva appears daily* (2.38.1).

7. *Rishis establish a relationship of Usha and Bhaga Devata with Savita* when they say that Savita appears after Usha (5.81.2) and before Bhaga Devata (5.82.3, 7.38.1). A relationship is also established with Surya when Rishis say that Savita combines with the rays of Surya (5.81.4).

   All this goes to show that Usha, Savita and Bhaga are close with each other, they come on earth one after another and they have a close association with Surya also.

8. Rishi Vishwaavasurdevagandharva informs that Surya Deva resides in Surya circle or zone or solar system (10.139.2). This again establishes a close relationship between the two.

9. Rishi Shyaavaashva Aatreya establishes a *relation between Savita Deva and Mata Aditi* (5.82.6). Rishi Vasishtha adds that Savita Devata is adored by Varuna, Mitra, Aryaman and other gods because the divine Aditi, delighted at the birth of the divine Savita, glorifies him (7.38.4).

   Rishis, it is clear, are establishing a relationship amongst Mother Aditi and other Aadityaas like Varuna, Mitra, Aryaman etc. Does it not prove that Rishis are saying that Savita is also an Aaditya?

10. Rishi Shyaavaashva Aatreya says that Savita Deva is rays of Surya (5.81.4). He further reveals that Savita Deva is yellow. His hairs are yellow (10.139.1), his eyes are golden (1.35.8), his tongue is golden (6.71.3), his hands are golden (1.35.9, 10, 6.71.4), his Varna (colour) is golden, his armour is golden (4.53.2) and his clothes are yellow (4.53.2). Even his yoke of chariot is golden (1.35.5). Further, Savita approaches the Surya (1.35.9) and informs Surya that men are free from sin (1.123.3).

    All this description clearly establishes that Savita is of yellow colour Energy Rays of Surya or Mother Aditi and is also an Aaditya because he is able to plead with Surya that men are innocent or sinless.

    The above narration by Rishis, when studied with the help of science, establishes that Savita Deva, like other Aadityaas, is an Aaditya. Rishi Vasishtha confirms it when he establishes a relationship of Mother Aditi, Savita, Mitra, Aryaman, Varuna etc. (7.58.4). This means that because of Mother Aditi, the core part of Sun, called Photosphere, where continuous Nuclear Fusion is taking place, the various Energy Waves are reaching earth in three main Bands. The science adds that the middle Band of Energy waves consists of seven colour rays—Red, Orange, Yellow, Green, Blue, Indigo and Violet. They reach earth in the morning, one after another. The first to reach is Red colour ray followed by Orange, Yellow, Green, etc. and they also leave earth, at the time of sunset, in the reverse order. So Savita Deva must be a yellow colour Energy Rays coming in the morning and leaving in the evening.

Is it not surprising that the wise Rishis of Rig Veda could reveal these scientific facts, some 6000 years back, when science is finding them now, during the last two hundred years.

The question which remains unanswered is: How does Savita Deva purify waters and air (2.38.2, 6.71.1)? Let us take the help of science.

Science tells us that there are two energy Bands which are on both the sides of the Central Band having seven colour rays. One of them is Ultra-Violet Rays and the other is of Infra-Red Rays. Science further tells us that Infra-Red Rays Band is quite hot when the Ultra-Violet Rays are cold. The Central Band having seven colour rays has energy waves with different heat—the hottest being Red Rays and the coldest Violet Rays. So, yellow colour rays are quite hot. It is a well known principle of science that heat purifies water and air. So, Rishis were giving a scientific fact when they said that Savita Deva purifies water and air. Science also says that yellow colour also makes vision more clear. It is for this reason that in the operation theatre, yellow colour bulb is used.

Chapter 6

Bhaga Devata

Very little material is available on Bhaga Devata in Rig Veda and yet Maharshi Dayananda has given a great importance to this Devata.

The following Mantras are found in Rig Veda which have reference of Bhaga Devata:

	Mantra	*Rishi*	*Deity*
1.	1.50.8	Praskadva Kaandava	Surya
2.	2.27.1	Kurmo Gratsamada, Gratsamada	Aaditya
3.	7.41.2-6	Vasishtha	Bhaga
4.	8.18.3	Irimbidhi Kaandava	Aaditya
5.	9.114.3	Kashyap	Pavamaana Soma

It is worth knowing why so little material is available on Bhaga Devata specially when Maharshi Dayananda Saraswati has given this deity a great importance.

The following information is available in Rig Veda on Bhaga Devata:

1. Rishi Vasishtha opines that Bhaga Devata is the son of Aditi (7.41.2). So Bhaga Devata is an Aaditya who should have all the qualities of an Aaditya—light giver, illuminator and heat giver. Further, he should be closely associated with other Aadityaas—Surya. Mitra, Usha, Savita, Aryaman, Daksha, Ansha, Varuna and Indra.

2. Who is Mata Aditi and what are her qualities? A reading of Rig Veda reveals that Mata Aditi is light (4.25.3, 10.36.3). She has a lustre (7.82.10) and she has tremendous heat.

   Surya is also an Aaditya (1.191.9), son of Mata Aditi. He has light (1.7.3, 1.50.1, 4, 5; 10.120.1) and heat as he scorches the region (7.34.19). He has seven steeds (5.45.9). All this shows that the qualities of Surya Devata and Mata Aditi are alike.

   Scientific studies of Sun reveal that the Sun has two parts, inner part (Core Part) and outer part. In Core Part, called Photosphere, continuous Nuclear Fusion is taking place and Energy waves in three main Bands are going out. They reach earth also. The middle Band mainly consists of seven colour Energy Rays—Red, Orange, Yellow, Green, Blue, Indigo and Violet. These seven colour rays reach earth, one after another, in the morning and leave at the time of sunset in the reverse order.

   A comparison of Surya Devata and Mata Aditi with the scientific knowledge about Sun leaves no doubt that Mata Aditi is the core part of the Sun, i.e., Photosphere where Nuclear Fusion is taking place. And the seven steeds of Surya Devata are nothing but the middle Band of Energy Rays, generated in Mata Aditi, which is of seven colours.

Now the question is who are these seven steeds of Rig Veda? What are their names and to which colour do they belong?

The studies of the author have revealed:

1. That Mitra Devata is the Red colour Energy wave—First steed.
2. That Usha Devi is the Orange colour Energy wave—Second steed.
3. That Savita Deva is the Yellow colour Energy wave—Third steed.

So, the problem is to find out the colours of the other four steeds, viz., Bhaga, Aryaman, Daksha and Ansha who are also Aadityaas—children of Mother Aditi. An effort is being made here to find out the colour of Bhaga Devata, the subject of the present study.

Maharshi Dayananda Saraswati has said that prayers should be offered to Bhaga Devata at the time of Sunrise. Rishi Vasishtha also seems to say so (7.41.4). Before Sunrise, first comes the Red colour Rays followed by Orange colour, Yellow colour and Green colour rays. We have already identified Red, Orange and Yellow colour Rays. So, Bhaga must be a green colour Ray. Rishi Vasishtha prays "May the Dawn come to our sacrifice as a horse—as rapid steeds convey a chariot, so may the Dawns bring to us Bhaga, down descending, charged with riches" (7.41.60). So, it is clear that since Bhaga Devata appears just at the time of dawn, it should be a green colour ray. Science confirms it.

Chapter 7

More about Seven Colour Energy Rays of Surya

Rishis of Rig Veda have been chiefly mentioning the advantages which Surya Devata, specially his seven colour energy rays, viz., Mitra, Usha, Savita, Bhaga, Aryaman, Daksha and Ansha bestow on man. Taking clue from them, later Rishis have studied them in depth.

Scholars opine that there are four Vedas—Rig Veda, Yajur Veda, Saam Veda and Atharva Veda and there are four Up-Vedas, one connected with each Veda. Up-Veda connected with Rig Veda is Ayur Veda (Medical science connected with Anatomy, Pharmacology, Medicine, Paediatrics, Medicinal Chemistry etc.) and Rishi Dhanvantri is said to be the author of a very important treatise known as SUSRUTA. The other important and authentic treatise is CHARAK written by Agnivesh.

Ayur Veda has taken clue from Rig Veda.[1] Some important references from Rig Veda:

1. 8.72.16—"The wind by means of the Sun's seven rays milks the nourishing food and drink from the seven stepped one."

   Obviously, this means that the seven colour rays of the Sun give seven types of energy. They are, as per science, Red, Orange, Yellow, Green, Blue, Indigo and Violet.

2. 4.50.14—"Brihaspati, when first being born in the highest heaven of supreme light, seven mouthed, multiform, (combined) with sound, and seven rayed, has subdued the darkness."

   Here again, the importance of seven rays of the sun is revealed.

3. 5.45.9—"May Surya, lord of seven steeds, arrive, for he has a distant goal (to reach) by a tedious route: fleet as a hawk he pounces upon the offered (sacrificial) food: ever young and for seeing, he shines , moving amidst rays of light."

   The importance of seven colour energy rays is highlighted here also.

Atharva Veda takes note of these seven colour energy rays of the Sun and in Mantra 1.1.1 opines that the permutation and combination of these seven colour energy rays produce 21 rays which are of great importance to human beings.

---

[1]Pt. Hari Prapanna Sharma, Rasa-Yoga-Sagar, vol. 1, Published by the author himself, Printed at Karnatak Printing Press, Bombay, 1927 has quoted 157 verses from the Vedas to show how much the Ayur Veda is indebted to the Vedas, pp. 28, 32-61.

Science tells us that these seven colour rays of the sun have different wavelengths and frequencies[2] and they reach earth, one after another, in the morning and leave earth in the evening in the reverse order. When all of them are on earth, together, they produce white colour. Thus, science seems to hold the theory of Rishis of Atharva Veda that the seven rays produce a number of combinations and play an important role in human life.

Ayur Veda, which is a sub-Veda of Rig Veda, says that there are five basic elements—Earth (Prithvi), Air (Vayu), Water (Varuna), Fire (Agni or Surya) and Sky (Aakaasha). All the material things are born out of the permutation and combination of these five basic elements. Science agrees with this. From this, it can easily be inferred that the cause of illness of a man is the imbalance of these five elements. Out of these five elements, Rishis opine, earth and water should be considered as the least important. So the remaining three are active elements. They are, in the terminology of Rishis: *Vaata* (Air or Gas), *Pitta* (Bile or Fire) and *Kafa* (Phlegm or Eather). They say that they are at the root of most of the diseases. So, restoring back the balance will cure the

---

2

	Energy Ray	*Wavelength*	*Frequency*
1.	Red (Mitra)	6.1×10^{-7} to 7.8×10^{-7}	4.06×10^{14}
2.	Orange (Usha)	5.9×10^{-7} to 6.1×10^{-7}	4.91×10^{14}
3.	Yellow (Savita)	5.7×10^{-7} to 5.9×10^{-7}	5.08×10^{14}
4.	Green (Bhaga)	5.0×10^{-7} to 5.7×10^{-7}	5.16×10^{14}
5.	Blue (Aryaman)	4.5×10^{-7} to 5.0×10^{-7}	6×10^{14}
6.	Indigo (Daksha)	4.0×10^{-7} to 4.5×10^{-7}	6.67×10^{14}
7.	Violet (Ansha)	4.0×10^{-7} to 4.5×10^{-7}	7.5×14^{14}

disease. Ayur Veda says that vegetation, which has these three elements in abundance, can be a good source of medicines. So reliance was put on medicines prepared with herbs, having the required properties.

Ayur Veda has grouped the seven colour energy waves of the Sun in three broad groups, probably on the basis of their properties and tried to synchronise them with the three basic elements which are mainly responsible for. various diseases. These groups and their basic elements are:

	Sun Rays	*Basic Element*
Group I	Red, Orange and Yellow	*Kafa* (Phlegm or Eather)
Group II	Green	*Vaata* (Air or Gas)
Group III	Blue, Indigo and Violet	*Pitta* [Bile or Fire (Agni)]

Ayur Veda has given a list of diseases caused due to the imbalances (excess or shortage) of each of these basic elements. It broadly tells that eighty diseases can be caused by imbalance of *Vaata* (Gas), forty by *Pitta* (Bile or Agni), and twenty by *Kafa* (Phlegm or Eather).

Basic properties of these three elements are given in the table below.

Table No. 1[3]
Properties of Three Variables

S. No.	*Vaata* (Gas)	*Pitta* (Bile)	*Kafa* (Phlegm)
1.	It affects that part of the body	It affects that part of the body where	It affects mainly upper or lower

	where air is needed, i.e., *Pran Vayu*—heart, lungs etc.	*Pran* Energy is found (generation of electricity is done) such as navel, cells, pace maker in heart etc.	part of the body which has holes such as ears, nose etc.
2.	It induces cold	It induces heat	It does not induce
3.	It is thin	It is thick	It is thick
4.	It can expand or contract	It is fluid	It is sticky, cannot easily expand or contract
5.	It is light, i.e., easily digestible	It is light	It is heavy, i.e., difficult to digest
6.	It is dry	It is oily	It is slippery

Ayur Veda is of the opinion that the three groups of coloured energy waves of the Sun can help in curing the three groups of diseases. For example, if a person is suffering with *kafa* (Phlegm) and takes a bath in the sun rays of Red, Orange and Yellow colours, he is bound to be cured. The duration and timing of this Ray's Bath will depend on the time factor, viz., when these waves reach the spot and for how long they are affective at that place. They are effective twice—in the morning when they come and in the evening when they leave. Probably, it was this reason why wise Rishis provided *Sandhya* twice in the day, i.e., morning and evening. Arya Samaj has patronised it.

[3] *Charak Samhita* and also *Vag Bhatta* written by Vag Bhatta, Nirnay Sagar Press, Bombay, Ch. XI.

Today Allopathy has developed techniques to treat patients by artificial Radiation Therapy of various colour rays such as Ultra-Violet Rays. Besides this, Sun bathing has become a fashion in West mainly in cold countries.

This proves that what Rishis of Rig Veda said earlier was developed later by the Rishis of Ayur Veda and medical science discovered it in the nineteenth century.

ANOTHER DEVELOPMENT: JEWEL THERAPY

Wise men of India, on the basis of the scentific knowledge about seven colour energy waves of the Surya Devata, developed another scientific way of treatment, called Jewel Therapy. This therapy has become immensely popular in India though people do not know the scientific knowledge behind it.

The wise Rishis made, at a period of time, an intensive study, to know the effect of the seven planets—Sun, Moon, Mars, Mercury, Jupiter, Venus, Saturn, Rahu and Ketu on man, the place and the atmosphere.[4]

These Rishis cum scientists observed that each planet (like Sun) has its characteristics and powers and so the children born under its direct influence (i.e., when it is exactly above on the spot) are influenced by the characteristics of that planet. Otherwise also, each planet exerts its influence when it is nearer the object.

[4]The science of Horoscope is based on it.

Studies of Indian Rishis revealed that a child born under direct influence of a planet is likely to get beneficial effect of that planet and also its bad effects like getting diseases connected with that particular planet. They discovered, for example, that the children born under the direct influence of the Sun are likely to suffer from heart troubles and diseases connected with bones, lungs and stomach. Thus, they prepared a list of diseases connected with each planet.

The researches of Rishis revealed that the various precious stones have different chemical properties. Some examples are:

Ruby (Maanikya)	:	Aluminium, Oxygen
Pearl (Moti)	:	Calcium, Magnesium, lron and Cobalt
Coral (Moonga)	:	Calcium, Carbon, Oxygen
Emerald (Panna)	:	Beryllium, Aluminium, Silicon, Oxygen
Diamond (Heera)	:	Carbon
Topaz (Phukraj)	:	Aluminium, Silicon, lron, Hydrogen, Oxygen

The modern science confirms it.

Anatomy of a human body tells us that alum and medium veins supply blood to the fingers on the palm side of the hand. Similarly, Radium veins supply blood to the fingers on the reverse side of the palm. Rishis, in their own way, had discovered this fact, long back.

Contact Theory and Radiation Theory of Physics and Geology suggest that the basic elements in these jewels may pass on in the blood vessels of the fingers either by contact or radiation. Physicists have made some studies on these jewels by passing Sun Rays through them. They found out the life-span of a jewel, when used, is between 3 to 7 years. The wise Rishis had discovered it long back.

It appears the wise Rishis cum medico-men, by themselves, had discovered these facts. So, they advised people to wear one of these precious stones connected with the disease, in a prescribed finger to ward off the evil influence of a planet.

It will be worthwhile to take a definite case.

The Rishis observed that a person born under the influence of the Moon is likely to be more prone to diseases like mental and heart disorders, stones in kidney or gall-bladder, piles and small-pox. Science has yet to explore it and confirm or reject it.

To ward off the evil influence of the Moon, or to cure the patient, Rishis cum scientists cum medico-men prescribed that the patient should wear Pearl (Moti) of a minimum weight of four *Ratti* in a silver ring (which has also a radiation effect) in the left hand finger. They said, the effective life of this pearl is three years.

The modern Pathies of treatment, in a heart case, have this to say:

1. **Allopathy** tells us that cholesterol is one of the causes of the heart trouble. Calcium is quite effective in

reducing cholesterol content of the veins. So calcium is prescribed to the patient.

2. **Ayur Veda** provides pearl based medicine for heart patients.

3. **Homoeopathy** prescribes calcarious phos and magnesium phos to the heart patients and this is what pearl contains.

4. **Unani System**[5] prescribes Calcium, Zinc and Magnesium to the heart patients.

Thus, it is clear that Jewel Therapy is also giving same medicine to a patient which other Pathies prescribe.

The important thing to be noted here is that wearing of a jewel in a finger becomes effective because one of the Rays of the Sun helps its contents to pass on in the blood vessels of the finger and from there it goes in blood. Hence, importance of the finger, stone and the Sun Rays.

COLOUR THERAPY

Probably taking clue from Rishis of the importance of seven colour Energy Rays of the Sun in curing diseases, westerners developed another method of treatment based on Sun Rays Therapy. They take seven bottles of seven colours—Red, Orange, Yellow, Green, Blue, Indigo and Violet. If the bottles of seven colours are not available they

[5]Hamdard Research Centre, Delhi has published a book in which it has been said that Magnesium, Zinc and Calcium are very useful in the treatment of heart diseases.

take bottles of three colours (i) Red or Orange or Yellow, (ii) Green, and (iii) Blue or Indigo or Violet. They fill water in these bottles leaving a portion empty. Tight cork is put on the bottles. Then they are left in open where Sun Rays can easily reach. The medicine is ready after a few hours' radiation of Sun Rays.

Medical science accepts that it is as effective as Sun Rays of the different colours. Further, medical science has started using these seven colour rays in fomenting various parts of the body. Not only this, they have prepared medicines or instruments with the help of these rays also. For example, a company HOLOGENIX is making a fibre. This fibre is made from a blend of polyester and finely ground minerals and gem-stones. This fibre supposedly works by channelling both ambient light and the energy a body generates in a way that increases the oxygen level of the blood flowing to the body parts it covers. It is said to relieve aches and pains with a simple sock or glove (Hindustan Times, New Delhi, Dt. 26.12.2003).

Summing up, one can conclude that the seven colour Energy Waves of the Sun have beneficial effect on human beings. Rishis of Rig Veda could discover it and later Rishis could apply it in different ways to prevent or cure diseases.

Chapter 8

Other Agni Devatas

The Rishis of Rig Veda, as is generally held, resided in the North-West of India now known as Sindh (Pakistan), Punjab (Pakistan and India), Haryana (India) and some parts of Rajasthan (India).

It is difficult to precisely say at what period the art of lighting Agni was discovered but a guess can be ventured. Probably, it was a period when nomad tribes, with their tame animals, had settled down, under the open sky, in a circular form, in open fields. In such a set-up, naturally the ladies, the children, animals and the old and weak stayed at the centre. Then, slowly, the art of making huts was invented and thereby whole tribe got splitted into innumerable households. People had also learnt the art of growing various crops. In the absence of an alternative to Sunlight, the whole life came to a standstill after the Sunset. The fear of wild animals and attacks from enemies and poisonous insects at night time also increased. In such a situation, one can visualize the importance of something which may provide, like Sun, the light and heat. Naturally learned people, called Rishis, were in search for such an alternative.

A.A. Macdonell, in his Vedic Mythology, has opined that in Rig Veda, Agni has been given an importance next to Indra. It is also credited with being the pivot of Hindu Sanskars, Hindu Culture and Hindu Civilization. No Sanskar, out of sixteen, can be performed without lighting Agni and performing *Havan*. Hence, it can be said that even today, Agni continues to be the central part of Hindu Culture and Civilization.

Reading of Rig Veda reveals that Vedic Rishis were scholars par excellence who had a deep and unified knowledge of all modern subjects like all branches of science, sociology, politics, economics, psychology, art etc. This they probably got by observing Mother Nature closely and trying to know its secrets. These wise, observant Rishis, in a period of time, bit by bit, discovered three types of Agni. An effort is being made here to describe these three types of Agni, one by one.

I. AGNI ON LAND

Rishis, who were keen observers of Nature, observed that when a strong wind moves, due to friction created between the dry branches of trees, shrubs and other vegetation, sparks of Agni are released. Dry branches of trees, shrubs and other vegetation catch this spark and big fire starts. This fire, Rishis observed, had twin qualities of the Sun, viz., light and heat. This forest fire they called *Davagana.* Thus, they got a clue to light Agni which can be an alternative to Sun, after Sunset.

Rishi Paraashar Shaakatya reveals that Agni was born in forests (R.V. 1.67.1). He further says that friction of two pieces of wood causes a spark of Agni (1.62.8). Rishi Agni Saucheek, Rishi Vaishwaanara and Rishi Saptirvaarjabhar jointly confirm it (10.79.7). After this observation, naturally the next course would have been to ignite Agni by rubbing two pieces of wood. Different woods have different qualities of fibres. Therefore, a search for a right type of wood with the right type of fibre should have followed. Rishi Aangirasa was lucky in selecting such a wood (1.31.11). For this reason, Rishi Aangirasa is called the Father of Agni (1.31.11). There is no dearth of instances where by rubbing two pieces of wood, Agni was lighted (1.60.1, 1.68.2, 2.10.3, 3.23.2, 3.29.1, 5.6.3, 10.79.4).

Soon a problem might have arisen. After lighting a piece of wood, the question would have arisen how to keep this Agni burning because soon this piece of wood is reduced to ashes and Agni gets extinguished. A solution was not difficult to find. Rishi Medhaatithi Kaandava says that Agni was kept alive with Agni (1.12.6), i.e., after the spark of Agni is generated, to keep this Agni burning, the help of shrubs, other vegetation and dry wood was taken. This dispensed with the need of rubbing two pieces of wood repeatedly to light Agni. But this also necessitated keeping a heap of woods near at hand. Naturally this Agni was lighted at a central place of the residential area and so the heaps of woods were also stored there. In course of time this led to the invention of a *Havan-kund* which made it possible for individuals to keep their residential places lighted during the night time.

A search for a material which might help a piece of wood to easily catch the spark of Agni ignited by rubbing two pieces of wood started. Further, a search for a material which may increase the flames of Agni to make it more bright and warm, must have also started.

By this time, people had known the art of converting milk into curd and taking out butter from it. So, Rishis experimented with butter for both the things. Their experiments showed that butter is helpful in both the things but because of more water content, it is not very effective in the beginning. So, efforts were made to reduce water content in butter. Agni was helpful here also. The butter was converted into *Ghee* which performed both the purposes better. Rishi Medhaatithi Kaandava says that Agni is inflamed with the help of *Ghee* (1.12.5). Several Rishis of Rig Veda say that *Ghee* helps better in igniting Agni and increasing its flames (2.7.4, 3.21.1, 5.11.3, 10.69.2).

The discovery of Agni and invention of *Ghee* helped in several ways:

1. After sunset the human activity used to come to a standstill. The discovery of Agni and invention of *Havan Kund* and *Ghee* helped in making life a little more active and comfortable at night time. Rishi

Paraashar Shaakatya informs that Agni, like Sun, is a giver of light, it is illuminating and destroyer of darkness. It perfects the earth (1.69.1). Several Rishis express similar views (1.1.8, 1.26.2, 1.58.3, 1.66.1, 1.94.5, 1.140.1, 1.149.3, 2.10.2, 4.8.2, 5.1.11, 5.7.4, 6.4.5, 8.43.32, 10.8.2, 10.91.4, 5).

2. Agni becomes a protector of houses and living beings (1.74.2). Wild animals and poisonous insects like snakes keep themselves away because of Agni (1.76.3, 3.10.2). It also saves from the attacks of enemies and evil doers at night as they get exposed due to the light of Agni (1.12.5, 3.15.1,10.87.2, 3, 5, 14). For this protective role of Agni, it is called RAKSHOHAN (10.87.1). Rishi Gautama Raahugana summarises by saying that Agni makes YAJMAN strong and brave (1.74.8).

3. After the discovery of Agni, HAVAN and YAGYA, twin pivots of Hindu culture, came into existence. The Rig Veda is full of Rishis performing HAVAN or YAGYA, inviting various deities and requesting them to help them in innumerable ways.

4. Discovery of Agni helped in boiling milk, which proved to be a better preserver of milk, specially in summers. Similarly, boiling butter and converting it into *Ghee* proved to be not only a better preserver but also a better inflamer of Agni. So, henceforth, sacrifices in Agni were made with *Ghee* in place of butter.

5. Rishis after Rishis say that Agni deity is media of not only inviting other deities but also to bring them to the place of HAVAN (6.1.1, 6.4.1, 6.11.6, 6.16.1,

7.3.7, 8.23.8, 8.44.9, 20). Explaining it, they say that Agni, through smoke, goes to sky, contacts various deities residing there, and gives them invitation (1.1.2, 1.12.3, 1.75.5). He carries HAVI to deities (5.25.4). Thus, Agni is said to be a friend to various deities (1.127.4). He becomes their messenger (5.11.4, 5.21.3). This means that Agni is a go between man and deities and so manages their blessings for human beings. *This should mean that other deities were born prior to Agni.*

6. When Agni was considered a friend of several deities, who brings them where HAVAN is being performed and gets several types of blessings from them for men, then slowly he also acquired all the qualities of a deity himself. For example, he started giving wealth (2.1.10, 3.13.4, 3.18.3, 5.6.9, 5.25.7, 6.16.5, 7.1.2, 3, 5), corn (1.73.5, 2.1.10, 3.20.2, 4.10.6, 4.11.3, 5.4.1, 5.6.9, 6.1.4, 7.3.1), animals (5.24.1, 2), sons (7.1.4, 5, 8.23.21) and whatever one asked for (3.15.6).

7. Various Rishis revealed one more property of Agni. Rishi Deerghatamaa Auchathya establishes a relationship between Agni and medicines which help in purifying the atmosphere. He reveals that Agni acquires (i.e., burns) medicines, i.e., medicinal plants. He becomes strong because of consuming these medicines. He becomes full of vigour and godly virtues. Thereafter, Agni and medicines, i.e., medicinal plants purify the earth and sky, i.e., atmosphere (1.140.7). Rishi Vimad Aindra, Rishi Prajaapati and Rishi Vasukridwasukra jointly go one step forward and say that Agni provides seeds to medicines, i.e., helps in growth of medicinal plants

(10.21.8). Rishi Vasishtha confirms it by saying that Agni, in form of corn, i.e., seed, enters medicinal plants (7.9.2, 3). A strong relationship is established between Agni, medicinal plants and purification of atmosphere.

This view of Rishis appears plausible because even today certain crops are burnt after cutting. The sugarcane crops, to make new crops strong and better, are burnt after harvesting. And, science admits that Agni is a great purifier of the atmosphere. It burns all the insects etc. in the atmosphere or bad plants on the earth.

8. In course of time, Agni helped in melting various metals and thereby helped in giving them a different form. This helped in developing several crafts which produced a variety of consumer and capital goods. For example, Gai Aatreya informs that craftsman increases Agni flames in ovens (5.9.5). Rishi Bharadwaajo Vaarhaspatya informs that goldsmiths melt gold (6.3.4). Mention is found of *Vajra* of Indra made of iron (1.81.4) and some *Vajras* made with several joints, to give them length, and sharp edges to enable them to cut more efficiently (6.17.10, 6.22.6).

9. Agni was used in one more important way. Mention is found in Rig Veda where dead were left in open field, there being no method to dispose of the dead bodies. Mention is also found that dead bodies were buried. But after the discovery of Agni, a more scientific method of disposing of the bodies was invented by burning them. Rishi Damno Yaamaayan prays Agni not to give pain to the dead (while

burning him) and not to scatter his various parts. Prayer is also made to take him to his forefathers (10.16.1).

OTHER FORMS OF AGNIS ON EARTH

After the successful discovery of lighting Agni by rubbing two pieces of wood, efforts were made to inflame Agni by rubbing other things also. It is worthwhile to mention a few such efforts here.

1. Efforts were made to generate Agni by friction of stones. Rishi Vimad Aindra, Rishi Prajaapati and Rishi Vasukridwasukra name this Agni as son of stones as it was produced by the friction of stones (10.20.7). Since it was a more taxing method, it could not obviously become popular.

2. Agni was also generated by the friction of metals. Rishi Deerghatamaa Auchathya reveals that Agni resides in metals also (1.41.3). But this method was also a difficult process and so obviously could not become popular.

All this description by Rishis of finding Agni in wood, stones & metals is testified by the modern science also.

Some Rishis gave a picturesque description of the burning of shrubs, vegetation, trees etc. by Agni. Rishi Deerghatamaa, in a poetic way, describes that Agni proceeds eating twigs, vegetation, medicinal plants etc. which are akin to clothes of mother earth. Thereafter, Agni leaves behind a black path (1.140.9). Rishi Saumaahuti agrees (2.4.6) and Rishi Vasishtha confirms it (7.3.2).

It appears efforts have been made by some Rishis to give a spiritual twist to the discovery of Agni in wood. Rishi Kumar Aatreya and Rishi Vrisho Jaar say that just like an expectant mother keeps the child in her womb similarly logs of wood keep Agni in their womb (5.2.2). Rishi Vasishtha agrees (7.5.9).

This concept of Agni and the other concept of Agni, viz., a spark of Agni is created by friction of wood, stone, metal etc. are not akin.

II. AGNI IN WATERS

Observant Rishis of Rig Veda observed that continuously innumerable rivers are bringing water and depositing it in ocean and yet the banks of ocean remain intact. They are not submerged with water. This observation forced them to find out what happens to this river water. Soon they discovered that a huge Agni is burning below the ocean. The Agni and the Sun Agni evaporate the ocean water. They called it BADVAGNI. Rishi Vishwaamitra Gaathin opines that Agni is in BADVANAL (3.7.3). He further opines that gods discovered Agni in the water of rivers (3.1.3). Rishi Paraashar Shaakatya reveals that Agni is born out of womb of water (1.65.2). Rishi Deerghatamaa agrees (1.143.1, 1.144.2). Maatrishvaa took out Agni by churning water (1.141.3). Rishi Budha Aatreya says that Agni is in water (5.1.6). Rishi Viroop Aangirasa (8.43.9) and Rishi Vatsa Prirbhaalandan (10.45.3) describe this in their own way.

The modern science testifies both the observation of the ancient Rishis, viz. (1) Agni is burning in the core of the earth, below the ocean, which causes water evaporation. Rishis called it BADVAGNI. (2) Water contains Agni. They say that water can also help in generating hydro-electricity.

III. AGNI IN SKY

Rishis were keen observers of Mother Nature. They observed that during the rainy season, there is a flash of light which resembles Agni. It sometimes falls on earth with a loud noise. When it falls on earth it reduces the objects to ashes. It, like Agni of earth, is white, illuminating, giver of light and capable of burning things. They started calling this Agni as Apaam-Napaat (2.35). Elaborating, Rishi Vishwaamitra Gaathin points out that sky Agni resides in the sky womb of sky water, i.e., clouds (3.1.11). He further says that this sky Agni resides between sky and earth (3.6.4). Modern science agrees and says that clouds do not go beyond Toposphere, i.e., a height of 10 miles.

There seems to be a difference of opinion about where Agni was first found. In the opinion of Rishi Vatsaprirbhaalandan Agni was first born in sky (10.45.1).

Rishi Gratsamada gives a full Sukta on Sky Agni, which is dedicated to Apaam Napaat (2.35). He calls them as the grand children of water. According to him, because of BADVANAL (i.e., the fire below the ocean) the sea water evaporates and the clouds are formed which surround Apaam Napaat, i.e., Sky Agni (2.35). Rishi Deerghatamaa opines that Sky Agni is born in clouds and describes them (1.143.1,

2, 3). Rishi Bharadwaajo Vaarhaspatya is definite that Sky Agni, i.e., Apaam Napaat is white, resident of sky, ageless and noisy. They are friend to Maruta-Gan i.e. wind (6.6.2). We find many Mantras on the subject (7.9.3, 8.44.29, 10.187.5).

CONCLUSION

A reading of Agni in Rig Veda reveals several things viz.

1. The observant Rishis were successful in finding out all the three types of Agni—on the ground, in the water and in the sky. They were also successful in making several uses of Agni of land for the welfare of man . They could also differentiate between the Agni and the heat and light generated by the Sun due to nuclear fusion.

2. Agni has been shown as a friend of other gods, a media to invite them for the welfare of man. So, to make the innovation perfect, Agni has been provided with horses (1.58.2) or even equated with a horse (1.149.2, 6.12.6, 1.60.5, 7.7.1, 2.5.1, 3.26.4, 3.27.14, 3.26.3, 4.2.8). He has also been associated with birds (7.15.4, 1.164.92). All this is to prove his powers to move anywhere freely and quickly and thereby complete his missions easily.

3. With a view to create a psychological effect on human beings so that they may worship Agni, live in tune with Agni and may not misuse it, Agni was not only raised to the status of a deity but also provided a human form, on the basis of its qualities. Here are some examples. Agni has:

(1) GRIHIT-MUKH—One who eats Ghee or whose mouth is oily (3.1.18).

(2) GRIHIT-KAISH—Whose flames resemble hairs (8.60.2).

(3) JWALA-KAISH—Whose hairs are like flames (1.45.6).

(4) HARIT - KAISH—Probably, colour of some flames may appear to be green (3.2.13).

(5) TRI-JAVVAHA—Flames get splitted into three and so they are called three tongues (3.20.2).

(6) SAHASRA-NETRE—One who can see everywhere (1.79.12).

(7) HARI-DAADHI—(Green Beard) Probably to complete human picture (5.7.7).

(8) TEEKSHAN-JABDE—(Sharp Jaws) To help in eating, i.e., burning everything (8.49.3).

(9) HIRANYA -DANTA—(Golden Teeth) Signifying capacity to eat anything (5.2.3).

(10) LOHA-DANTA—(Steel Teeth) Signifying powers to chew and reduce everything to ash (10.87.2).

4. To increase the importance of Agni, it is shown as possessing three Gunas (10.88.10); three types of light (3.26.7), three heads (1.146.1), three figures and three bodies (3.20.2).

5. With passage of time, Rishis of *Ayur Veda*, which is a sub-Veda of Rig Veda, could find out thirteen types of Agnis in the body. One of these Agnis, called

JATHRAGNI, is responsible for the digestion of the food that we eat.

The above description of Agni clearly shows that Agni Devata is a Natural Phenomenon. So, it is omnipresent, omnipotent and beneficial to man. It is, therefore, desirable that human beings should try to know the secrets of this powerful god, i.e., the natural laws of all types of Agnis and should try to tune their lives in accordance with these natural laws. This is the real meaning of worshipping the god Agni.

Chapter 9

Devata Ashvins (Twin Gods)

47 Rishis of Rig Veda, i.e., 11.7% have offered 51 Suktas and 116 Mantras to Ashvins (they are two gods). The list of Suktas and Mantras is Appendix A.

A reading of these Suktas and Mantras clearly gives the impression that information about Ashvins could be gradually collected by these Rishis and upto the last, full information could not be found out. Why?

Whatever has been revealed by these Rishis about Ashvins is presented below in a systematic manner:

1. It has been said that Ashvins are a god (4.15.9, 10) but it has not been cleared why have they been called an Ashva, i.e., a horse. Is it because of the speed with which they move? Rishis reveal that they move with a great speed (1.180.2, 1.183.1, 4.75.5). They add that

they can move even with a speed of a thought (8.22.6).

2. Rishis opine that Ashvins are a great donor. It appears, therefore, that Rishis invite them to come to their Yagya, freely drink Soma and give them various things (5.75 to 5.79). They demand from them food (5.79.7, 8; 1.91.16, 17), wealth (1.92.19; 5.75.3, 5.76.5; 7.59.7), honey (7.77.3); horses (7.78.5, 10; 1.91.20), other animals (7.79.7, 8), milch cow (1.91.20), children (5.76.5, 1.91.20, 5.76.5) and their protection (5.77.4). The Ashvins freely grant them their prayers and also protect them from enemies (1.91.23), kill their enemies (1.91.18) and give them rainfall (1.91.21). They seem to be all powerful.

   Similar things have also been said about other gods. So it does not help in identifying Ashvins.

3. It has been said by the Rishis that Ashvins are two gods. To give this idea Ashvins have been compared with those men, animals or birds who are in two. For example, two buffaloes (8.35.7), two geese (8.35.8), two weavers (10.106.1), two horses (10.106.2), two wings of a bird (10.106.3) and like two mad elephants (10.106.6). A.A. Macdonell agrees.[1]

4. Rishis are not unanimous about the residence of Ashvins. For example Rishi Purimilla reveals, like other Rishis, that Ashvins travel round the heaven and beyond it (4.43.5). Some Rishis opine that they are grandsons of Heaven (1.182.1; 1.84.1, 4.44.2), i.e., by implication reside in Heaven. They came

[1]A.A. Macdonell, Vedic Mythology (Hindi version), Chaukhamba Vidya Bhawan, 1984, pp. 91-92.

from above the Heaven (1.46.3; 1.74.1). Rishi Paur Aatreya is inquisitive. He wants to know from where they come and where do they reside (5.74.2)? Do they reside at several places or do they reside in mid air (5.73.1)? Rishi Agastya Maitravaruni also enquires: where were they born? Were they born in the middle of the sky (i.e. from the area upto 300 miles above the earth which Rishis call Antariksha) or above it (where there is vacuum) or where solar system exists? No firm answer could be found out.

5. Rishis give special importance to Ashvins' chariot. They repeatedly describe it. They tell that it is made of gold (4.44.4, 5, 7.69.1), its supporting shaft, axle and both the wheels are of gold (8.5.29) and the decoration of the chariot is of gold (8.22.5). What does it mean? Does it show that Ashvins' chariot, like them, was also glittering or shining as the sun.

   The chariot of Ashvins has three wheels (1.34.2). It is of triangle shape (1.47.2, 1.139.4) and its sitting place has also three compartments (1.34.2, 7.69.2, 8.22.5, 8.86.8). Ashvins travel, while sitting in this chariot, three times in the day and three times in the night (1.34.2). They are worshipped three times (1.34.7). They distribute medicines three times (1.34.6) and do several works three times such as imparting three-fold knowledge, shower food thrice etc. (1.34.4, 5).

   Associating Ashvins with three must be with some specific purpose. What is this purpose? Scholars should find it out. The writer feels that in Hindu Dharma, three has been given a special importance. For example, trinity is of three gods—god Vishnu, god Rudra and god Brahma; there are three worlds—

Aakaasha (Sky), Prithvi (Earth), and Paataal (Below the earth); there are three Gunas—Satguna, Rajoguna and Tamoguna etc. (We will revert to it afterwards.)

6. Rishis opine that Ashvins are ancient gods (7.62.5).[2] But in spite of the fact that they are ancient, they always remain young (3.59.7, 7.67.10). In other words, they are not affected by time. They are immortal like every other god.

7. Ashvins are handsome (1.47.2, 6.62.5, 6.63.1) with white complexion (7.68.1), i. e., shining. In Rig Veda, almost all gods have been associated with these qualities.

8. Ashvins are strong (10.24.4), endowed with profound intellect (8.8.2) and hidden powers.[3] All the other gods of Rig Veda have similar qualities. This description of Ashvins does not help us, in identifying them and also differentiate them from other gods. Further, it is not clear whether there are any differences between both the Ashvins. So, with the help of science and other traits of Ashvins, efforts are being made to identify them.

9. Rishis describe both Ashvins illuminating (7.68.1) and invested with solar radiance (8.82). Thus, indirectly, both Ashvins have been associated with Mother Aditi or god Sun. This fact is confirmed by other Rishis who say god Usha awakens them (1.22.1, 1.92.18, 8.5.1, 8.9.17), or Ashvins come along with

---

[2]Op. cit., p. 92.
[3]Op. cit., p. 92.

dawn (7.67.2, 10.61.4) or before dawn (3.58.1), or after dawn (8.5.2). The time of Ashvins appearing on earth may be a disputable matter but their association with the Sun and Mother Aditi is confirmed. Several other Mantras also confirm this view (1.46.3, 1.47.7, 9; 1.92.17, 1.184.6, 1.119.1).

Rishi Surya Sautri provides a very important and meaningful clue when she reveals that the daughter of Sun, Suryaa, was married to Ashvins, i.e., both Ashvins. Sukta 10.85 gives a beautiful description of marriage.

Devata Soma, it is said, wanted to marry Suryaa but Suryaa selected Ashvins (10.43.6, 10.85.9). All the gods assented to it (10.85.14). Thereupon Ashvins said: "I take your hand for good fortune, that you may attain old age with me as your husband; the gods Bhaga, Aryaman, Savita, Purandh have given you to me; that I may be master of a household" (10.85.36).

This narration makes it abundantly clear that Devi Suryaa, seven colour rays of the Sun and Ashvins have a close relationship. What is this relationship? Let us take the help of science.

Science tells us:

1. That from the Sun, i.e., from the core of the Sun, whom Rishis have called Mata Aditi, different types of rays emit from the Sun.
2. That there are three main Bands of these Rays.
3. That the Central Band of rays is visible on the earth and has seven sub-bands of seven colour rays—Red, Orange, Yellow, Green, Blue, Indigo, and Violet. It appears, Rishis of Rig Veda, who

could find out these seven colour rays (as has been discussed earlier), have called this Central Band Devi Suryaa.

4. That on both the sides of this Central Band of rays, there are two other bands of rays which cannot be seen on earth by a man with the naked eyes; some of the rays coming from one of these bands are beneficial to man but the rays of the other bands are injurious.

5. That on one side are the Rays of Infra-Red Rays, Microwaves, Radio Waves and Long Radio Waves and, on the other side, are Ultra-Violet Rays, X-Rays and Gama Rays. These Rays can be shown with the help of the following diagram:

That with the help of this scientific information, it should not be difficult to identify Ashvins (plural). One Ashvin should be the band of Infra-Red Rays and the other Ashvin should be the band of Ultra-Violet Rays.

In these two bands of Rays, the band of Infra-Red Rays is very hot and the band of Ultra-Violet Rays is very cold. So, the seven colour rays of the middle band are of different heats—the Red Rays are the hottest and the Violet Rays are the coldest.

In support of this identification of Ashvins, i.e., both Bands of Rays, the following arguments can be given:

(i) Rishis reveal that Suryaa is the daughter of the Sun. They further reveal that the different colour rays came to see her off after marriage. This is a good way to describe a fact.

(ii) Rishis, at different places, have said that God Mitra (who is a Red Rays Band and should be, as explained by science, very hot) is a friend of god Indra and causes rainfall. Mitra, because of the heat of Red Rays, must be causing evaporation of water, which, at a particular height, should be taking the form of clouds and causing rain. This also confirms the views expressed about the friendship of the Varuna and the Mitra.

(iii) Rishis reveal that the Suryaa was married to two ever young, illuminating, identical young Ashvins. Indirectly they are saying that both Ashvins seem to be identical (because they could not be seen with the naked eyes from the earth). Further, to describe the location of Suryaa vis-a-vis Ashvins they give a beautiful description of the marriage of Suryaa with the two Ashvins.

10. Rishis reveal that Ashvins are wonderful Physicians (8.18.8, 10; 8.22.10). For example, they gave light to blind, enabled lame to walk, provided vigour to old,

cured the badly burnt and saved who had consumed lot of water on being drowned (1.112.6, 7, 8; 1.116.16, 8.18.10, 10.39.3, 8, 9, 10.41.7, 10.143.1). Today science is confirming the utility of Infra-Red Rays in curing various diseases which Rishis of Rig Veda revealed thousands of years earlier.

Thus, the science helps us not only in identifiying Ashvins but also to find out the difference between the two, which Rishis failed to do. Incidentally, this also solves the mystery of three wheeled and triangle shaped chariot of Ashvins having three compartments. It seems wise Rishis were referring in their own style, to the three bands of Rays—Infra-Red Rays, Seven Colour Rays and Ultra-Violet Rays.

APPENDIX A

SUKTAS AND MANTRAS ON ASHVINS

Sl. No.	*Suktas*	*Mantras*
1.	—	1.3.1, 2.3
2.	—	1.15.11
3.	—	1.22.1, 2, 3, 4
4.	—	1.30.17, 18, 19
5.	1.34	—
6.	1.46	—
7.	1.47	—
8.	—	1.92.16, 17, 18
9.	—	1.112.1, 2
10.	1.116	—
11.	1.117	—

12.	1.118	—
13.	1.119	—
14.	—	1.120.1-11
15.	—	1.139.3, 4, 5
16.	1.157	—
17.	1.158	—
18.	1.180	—
19.	1.181	—
20.	1.182	—
21.	1.183	—
22.	1.184	—
23.	2.39	—
24.	—	2.41.7, 8, 9
25.	—	3.39.3
26.	3.58	—
27.	—	4.15.9, 10
28.	4.43	—
29.	4.44	—
30.	4.45	—
31.	5.73	—
32.	5.74	—
33.	5.75	—
34.	5.76	—
35.	5.77	—
36.	5.78	—
37.	6.62	—
38.	6.63	—
39.	7.67	—
40.	7.68	—
41.	7.69	—

42.	7.70	—
43.	7.71	—
44.	7.72	—
45.	7.73	—
46.	7.74	—
47.	—	8.5.1-37
48.	8.8	—
49.	8.9	—
50.	8.10	—
51.	—	8.18.8
52.	8.22	—
53.	—	8.26.1-19
54.	8.35	—
55.	—	8.42.4, 5, 6
56.	8.57	—
57.	8.68	—
58.	8.73	—
59.	8.85	—
60.	—	8.101.7, 8
61.	—	10.24.4, 5, 6
62.	10.39	—
63.	10.40	—
64.	10.41	—
65.	10.61	—
66.	—	10.62.1-6
67.	—	10.85.6-13
68.	10.106	—
69.	—	10.131.4, 5
70.	10.143	—

Sky
(Aakaasha Devata)

Chapter 10

Aakaasha Devata (Sky)

Vedic Rishis have said that there are five basic elements whose permutations and combinations are responsible for the creation of all the material things and also sustaining them. One of these basic elements is Aakaasha, yet Rishs of Rig Veda have not offered even one full Sukta to Aakaasha Devata. Why?

Most of the Mantras or even Suktas on Aakaasha Devata have been offered jointly to Prithvi and Aakaasha. It will be beneficial to know the reasons for doing so.

We find following Mantras in Rig Veda offered to Aakaasha Devata along with others:

	Mantras	*Rishi*	*Deity*
1.	1.22.13.14	Medhaatithi Kaandava	Dhyaavaa, Prithvi
2.	1.94.16	Kutsa Aangirasa	Dhyausa, Prithvi,

			Mitra, Varuna, Aditi, Sindhu, Agni
3.	1.112.1	Kutsa Aangirasa	Dhyaavaa, Prithvi
4.	1.159	Deerghatamaa Auchathya	Dhyaavaa, Prithvi
5.	1.160	Deerghatamaa Auchathya	Dhyaavaa, Prithvi
6.	1.185	Agastya	Dhyaavaa, Prithvi
7.	2.32.1	Gratsamada	Dhyaavaa, Prithvi
8.	2.41.19, 20, 21	Gratsamada	Dhyaavaa, Prithvi, Havidata
9.	4.38.1	Vaamdeva	Dhyaavaa, Prithvi
10.	6.48.22	Shanyurvaarhaspatya	Dhyaavaa, Prithvi, Maruta
11.	6.70	Bharadwaajo Vaarhaspatya	Dhyaavaa, Prithvi
12.	10.59.9, 10	Viprabandhu Gopayana	Dhyaavaa, Prithvi

In addition to the above Mantras, two more Mantras provide very useful information.

1.	1.164.11, 18, 13	Deerghatamaa Auchathya	Vishvedeva
2.	10.68.11	Ayaasyu Aangirasa	Vrahaspati

Only nine Rishis of Rig Veda, out of all Rishis, i.e., 2% have offered their Mantras to Aakaasha Devata jointly with others, mainly with Prithvi. It is worth knowing the reasons why only nine Rishis have made studies of Aakaasha Devata?

It appears that Vedic Rishis either could not know more about Aakaasha Devata or there was nothing more to know. The latter seems to be more correct as the modern science is also not able to add any new information about Aakaasha authentically.

Following ideas in Rig Veda are found on Aakaasha Devata:

1. Rishi Deerghatamaa Auchathya reveals that Aakaasha and Prithvi were conceived in the same womb (1.159.4).The same Rishi also adds that the most divine Surya gave birth to the all- delighting Heaven (Aakaasha) and Earth (Prithvi) (1.160.4). So, it can be inferred that both Aakaasha and Prithvi are children of Surya. That may be the reason why most of the Mantras have been offered jointly to Aakaasha and Prithvi.

   Science reveals that a part of the Young Sun broke away from it, quite some time back, which is our Prithvi now . This scientific information confirms the Rishis' view given a few thousand years back.[1]

   Science does not tell us how Aakaasha came into existence. So, it may be presumed that when wise Rishi was correct in case of Prithvi, he may also be correct about Aakaasha. Aakaasha should also be a part of Sun (Surya).

2. Rishi Shanyurvaarhaspatya says that "once was the Heaven (Aakaasha) generated and once was the Earth (Prithvi) born (6.48.22). Rishis refer to Heaven (Aakaasha) but do not elaborate (6.51.5. 6.72.3). Thus, it appears that Aakaasha and Swarga (Heaven)

[1]Big Bang Theory which is yet in a hypothetic state, reveals that billions of years ago, the whole universe was concentrated in an infinitely small pointmass which exploded to give birth to all the galaxies, stars, etc. Our solar system is a part of it, so is our Sun and Earth. This theory also confirms the above statement of the Rishis.

are one and the same and are synonym and Swarga (Heaven) was also born out of Surya. This should mean (a) that Swarga (Heaven) is the area where Sun's solar system and his gravitation force exists, (b) that first from Sun, Heaven was born and thereafter the Earth.

3. Rishis offer their Mantras jointly to Dhyaavaa (Aakaasha) and Prithvi. It appears they knew that both were born simultaneously and are the children of the mighty Surya, having same properties. This knowledge seems to be the cause of offering Mantras jointly to them.

4. Rishi Deerghatamaa Auchathya says that Aakaasha is wide-spreading and vast (1.160.2) He adds the Antariksha is a part of Aakaasha (1.160.1). He further elaborates that Antariksha is the *nabhih* of earth, which is in between Heaven (Aakaasha) and Earth (Prithvi) (1.164.33). Rishi Gautamo Raahugana confirms it (1.90.7).

   Science tells us that above the Earth, towards Surya, there is air and gravitation pull of Prithvi upto 300 miles. Beyond it, is vacuum. It further tells that distance between the Sun and Earth is 9.3 crore miles. It means that the radius of Aakaasha (beyond Antariksha) is 9, 29, 99,700 miles (9,30,00,000 minus 300 miles). Certainly it makes Aakaasha wide and vast.

   It appears Rishis called Antariksha the area above the earth upto 300 miles, upto which air is found, and Aakaasha is the entire area within the radius of 9.3 crore miles which includes Antariksha also.

Thus, it can be concluded that Rig Veda has divided the entire universe into three domains:

(i) Lowest Domain—It consists of god Prithvi (Earth).

(ii) Middle Domain—It consists of atmosphere, i.e., upto 300 miles upward from earth where god Vayu (Air) and god Marudagan and god Indra reside.

(iii) Upper Domain—The zone above the level of atmosphere. It includes god Surya and the solar system. Rig Veda calls the upper and middle levels as god Aakaasha (Sky).

5. Rishis Bharadwaajo Vaarhaspatya states that the Heaven (Aakaasha) and Earth (Prithvi) are surrounded by water (6.70.4) but he did not explain or elaborate.

The science tells us that the Sun's core part, called Photosphere, has tremendous heat which is caused due to Nuclear Fusion going on there. It has gases also. The outer part, called Chromosphere is also very hot and has lot of gases. Science also informs that long back, a part of the Sun broke and today it is our Earth. Like Sun, it has also lot of gases. The mixture of few gases, long back, formed our oceans and water below the earth.

It appears Rishi is pointing out this scientific fact when he says that the Prithvi (earth) and Aakaasha (heaven) are surrounded by water. It Heaven is also a part of Surya, then as per scientific knowledge, it should also have lot of water.

6. Rishi Medhaatithi Kaandava reveals that in between Aakaasha and Prithvi there is the region of Gandharvas (1.22.14). This implies that in Aakaasha (Heaven) there is another region of Gandharva Loka or both are synonym. Science seems to be silent on this point.

7. Rishis tell that Aakaasha (Heaven or Dyuloka) is father and Prithvi (Earth) is the mother (1.159.2, 1.60.2, 1.164.33). They compare Prithvi (Earth) with a milch cow and Aakaasha (Heaven) with a vigorous bull (1.160.3). This means that Aakaasha is an active element and Prithvi is a passive element and all material things can be created only when the two meet. This is further certified by Rishi Agastya (1.185.5).

   Science agrees with this view of the Rishis when it says that nothing can grow on earth without the active help of other basic elements, specially sky.

8. Aakaasha has been called the father of all deities. Surya Deva is located in Aakaasha (1.164.18). The twelve spoked wheel, of the Surya, revolves round the heaven (1.164.11).[2] Further, Aakaasha (heaven) is decorated with constellations.[3]

Science agrees with Rishis. This shows the knowledge of the Vedic Rishis.

---

[2]The twelve spoked wheel are the twelve signs of the Zodiac—Aries, Taurus, Gemini, Cancer, Leo, Virgo, Libra, Scorpio, Sagittarius, Capricorn, Aquarius and Pisces. It may also mean twelve months of a year.

[3]Constellations are: Venus, Mercury, Sun, Mars, Jupiter, Saturn, Uranus, Neptune and Pluto.

The studies of Vedic Rishis convinced them that the twelve signs of Zodiac and nine constellations influence atmosphere and every material thing on earth, including man. On the basis of their (probably empirical) studies of Astronomy, they developed the science of Horoscope. Today modern science is gradually and haltingly agreeing to the view of Rishis. Today, they have started accepting its influence on atmosphere.

The modern science is not able to find more facts about sky or Aakaasha than what Rishis have said long back. They now only talk of a hypothetic matter, Eather.

Rishis, knowing the powers of Aakaasha and Prithvi, pray them to give horse and son (4.38.1), remove all inequity, let no ill approach them (10.59.9,10) and let their Yagya be performed peacefully (2.41.19).

Obviously there should be a reason for making such requests. Probably, Rishis wanted to convey the idea that if a man will follow the natural laws, will not try to exploit nature and will work in cooperation with nature, he will be happy and contented. Nature will grant him all the useful and necessary things of life.

Earth
(Prithvi Devata)

Chapter 11

Prithvi Devata (Earth)

According to Rig Veda all material things are created and sustained by the permutations and combinations of five basic elements—Agni (Surya), Aakaasha (Sky), Prithvi (Earth), Varuna (Water) and Vayu (Air). Naturally, Rishis of Rig Veda have attached good importance to Prithvi.

A.A. Macdonell considers Prithvi (Earth) as a Devata. Dr. Surya Kanta agrees with him.

It is surprising that on such an important Devata only one Rishi, Atri, offers a complete Sukta (5.84) while the other Rishis like Agastya, Kutsa Aangirasa, Gratsamada, Deerghatamaa Auchathya, Bharadwaaja, Vasishtha and Vipra Bandhu offer their Suktas or Mantras jointly to Prithvi and Aakaasha. There must be some valid reason for doing so. Efforts should be made to find it out.

Some important Mantras, found in Rig Veda concerning Prithvi Devata, are:

	Rishi	*Mantra*	*God*
1.	Agastya	1.174	Indra
		1.185	Dhyausa, Prithvi
2.	Atri	5.84	Prithvi
3.	Aivyaamrudaa Treyo	8.87.7	Maruta
4.	Kutsa Aangirasa	1.94.16	Prithvi, Dhyausa, Mitra,Varuna, Aditi, Sindhu
		1.112.1	Dhyaavaa, Prithvi
5.	Gratsamada	2.15.2	Indra
		2.32.1	Dhyaavaa, Prithvi
		2.41.19-21	Dhyaavaa, Prithvi
6.	Jamdagni (Rama)	10.110.9	Aapriya
7.	Deerghatamaa Auchathya	1.159	Dhyaavaa, Prithvi
		1.160	Dhyaavaa, Prithvi
		1.164.33	Vishvedeva
8.	Naaraayana	10.90.1, 13, 14	Purusha
9.	Bharadwaaja	6.70	Dhyaavaa, Prithvi
10.	Vasishtha	7.53	Dhyaavaa, Prithvi
		7.104.23	Prithvi, Antariksha
11.	Vaamdeva	4.17.4	Indra
		4.38.1	Dhyaavaa, Prithvi
		4.56	Dhyaavaa, Prithvi
12.	Vipra Bandhu	10.59.8, 9, 10	Dhyaavaa, Prithvi
13.	Shanyurvaarhaspatya	6.48.22	Dhyaavaa, Prithvi Maruta
14.	Shyaavaashva Aatreya	5.58.7	Maruta
15.	Savya Aangirasa	1.51 to 57	Indra
16.	Medhaatithi Kaandava	1.22.13.14	Dhyaavaa Prithvi

Out of all Rishis of Rig Veda only 16, i.e., 3.08% have contributed their views on Prithvi. One should know the reasons for it. Further, efforts should be made to know why most of the Rishis have offered their Mantras jointly to Dhyaavaa and Prithvi.

The compilation and systematisation of the material in Rig Veda on Prithvi Devata gave the following information.

ORIGIN OF PRITHVI

Rishi Naaraayana in Purusha Sukta reveals that Prithvi was born from the feets of Viraat Purusha (10.90.14). From this very Purusha Moon was born from the mind, the Sun from the eyes (10.90.13), Heaven from the head and Firmament (Antariksha) from the navel (10.90.14). This means that Prithvi, Moon, Sun, Heaven and Antariksha—all were born from the same source and they are closely related with each other, i.e., they must have similar properties.

Rishi Deerghatamaa Auchathya reveals that Aakaasha and Prithvi were born from the same place (1.159.4). This Rishi further adds that Surya gave birth to Heaven (Aakaasha) and Earth (Prithvi) (1.160.4). So, this Rishi, while agreeing with Rishi Naaraayana that both Prithvi and Surya have a common inheritance, adds that Prithvi is a child of Surya.

Rishi Agastya enquires: between Aakaasha and Prithvi, who was born first (1.185.1)? He does not answer this question but this also means that both were born from the same place.

Rishi Deerghatamaa Auchathya says that "the Heaven is my parent and progenitor; the Navel (of the earth) is my kinsman; the spacious Earth is my mother" (1.164.33).[1] It means that Aakaasha (Heaven) is an active element and Prithvi (Earth) is a passive element and probably Aakaasha is at the top. Antariksha (firmament) is below it and Earth is at the bottom.

The description of Rishis, by itself, does not give a clear picture of the origin of Prithvi and its location. So, let us seek the help of science.

Modern science reveals:

(i) The distance between the Earth and the Surya (Sun) is 9.3 crore miles.

(ii) Above the Earth, towards the Sun, upto 300 miles is air and gravitation pull of earth. Beyond this there is vacuum. In other words the region of Surya Devata starts. The Solar system is effective in this area and it is known as Aakaasha.

(iii) That about 500 crore years before, a part of the young Sun broke which is our Earth (Prithvi).[2]

The views of Rishis when read along with the above information given by the science show that what Rishis were saying some 6000 years ago science is saying today. Prithvi (Earth) is born out of Surya Devata. Further locationwise, above Prithvi, upto

---

[1]This Mantra has been offered to Vishwadeva.

[2]Modern Big Bang Theory also reveals that the Sun and the Earth have a common origin.

300 miles, is Antariksha and beyond that is Aakaasha, which also includes Antariksha.

CHARACTERISTICS OF PRITHVI

Rishis, in their own way, have given the following qualities or characteristics of Prithvi:

1. The size of Prithvi is quite big. Rishi Naaraayana opines "Purusha... investing the earth in all directions, exceeds (it by a space) measuring ten fingers" (10.90.1). Rishi Deerghatamaa says that Heaven (Aakaasha) and Earth (Prithvi) are widespread and vast (1.160.2). He asks "what is the uttermost end of the earth" (1.164.34) and seems to answer that it is endless (1.164.35).

   A.A. Macdonell opines that Prithvi means vast space. In his support he quotes Rishi Gratsamada Bhargava Shaunak (2.15.2).[3]

   Science reveals that Prithvi is like a ball whose diameter is 7926 miles long. This testifies the Rishis' view.

2. Rishi Atri says that Prithvi is strong like mountains and is mighty (5.84.1). Further, Prithvi because of her might, sustains the forest (5.84.3). This shows the structure and strength of Prithvi.

   Science reveals that Earth's core is made of rocks and solid metals like iron and other metals. The views of Rishis and science are one and the same.

---

[3]A.A. Macdonell, Vedic Mythology, Chaukhamba Vidya Bhawan, Varanasi, 1984, p. 167.

3. Rishi Vaamdeva reveals that because of the fear of Indra, Prithvi (Earth) trembled (4.17.2).

   Science agrees that the Earth shakes. It is because of earthquakes (not Indra).

   Rishis of Rig Veda say that the Earth shakes due to Agni.

   Science seems to agree. It says that since Earth is a part of the Sun, its inner part is still hot. Due to this heat, the metals and rocks get melted and so, at times, the mountains erupt lava and at other times Earth (melted rocks) moves.

4. Rishi Agastya says that "days (and nights) revolve as if they had wheels" (1.185.1). Rishi Atri says that Prithvi moves (5.84.2).

   Science tells us that Earth has two-fold movement. One, it revolves round the Sun and the other, it rotates round its axis. The movements give different seasons and day and night.

   The above description proves that what Rishis of Rig Veda were telling, about 6000 years before, about our Prithvi was all scientific truth. Present science has not been able to add to that knowledge.

5. Prithvi is fertile. Different Rishis say so in their own style. For example, Rishi Shyaavaashva Aatreya says that by the arrival of Marudagan, the fertility of Prithvi increases because "they deposit in her water as their germ, as the husband generates the embryo of the child" (1.58.7).[4] Rishi Atri, in his own way, supports the idea (5.84.1). Rishis Deerghatamaa

compares Prithvi with a mother (1.159.2) which also means she has fertility.

Science accepts the Earth is fertile.

6. Prithvi is kind-hearted. She gives happiness to all (1.160.1) and preserves the world (1.160.2). Rishis, due to Prithvi's generosity, pray her to give them wealth (1.185.3, 7.53.2).

   Scholars of today agree that Earth is kind-hearted and she returns multiple times than what she receives as seeds. All the economists, except Ricardo, agree that Mother Earth is fertile, kind-hearted and bountiful.

7. Prithvi is an essential element but she cannot do anything by herself. She is passive. Rishis say that Prithvi is mother and Aakaasha is father (1.159.2). Both together create and sustain all material goods.

   Science agrees. The economists say that Earth alone cannot produce anything by herself. It needs help of other essential elements like labour, capital, etc. Even minerals cannot be taken out without the help of labour.

8. Rig Veda gives a very important information about god Prithvi (Earth), viz., when god Prithvi (Earth) is one of the five elements, who creates all the material things, including human and other bodies, then it also helps in their disintegration. We get this idea in

---

[4]In Rig Veda the clouds are called Parjanya and the moving columns of air are called Marudagan. Probably the Rishis feel that without the help of Marudagan, Parjanya cannot give showers.

Sukta 10.18 of Rig Veda. It reveals that when the soul leaves the body, the human body becomes non-functional and is declared dead. What to do with this dead body? Rig Veda advises that the dead body should be taken to a place away from the village. Here the body should either be burnt (10.18.4) or buried (10.18.11, 12). In both cases, Mother Earth helps in the disintegration of the five basic elements (10.18.10), in one case immediately and in another case, slowly, in a period of time.

It appears Hindus first buried their dead but later took to burning because it disintegrates the body quicker and does not pollute the atmosphere like the other. This is because here god Agni (Fire), who is also one of the basic elements in creation, joins god Prithvi (Earth) and both are able to do the disintegration.

It is because of this importance of god Prithvi (Earth) that Hindus worship god Prithvi (Earth) and also love it like a mother. According to the author of these lines, the praying means:

(i) Worshipping god Prithvi (Earth) means that we try to know the laws of the Mother Earth (nature) and also try to tune our lives according to these laws. Living with nature should promote our mental peace and happiness.

(ii) Worshipping god Prithvi (Earth), as mother (because of her kindness, bountifulness and love), should mean that we should love and respect her intensely. When we love and respect Mother Prithvi like our own mother then it implies we love its mountains, valleys, planes, deserts, nay, its every particle (we make different gods out of our earth and stones and also make different parts of our Tirtha (religious places) and are prepared to sacrifice everything for her safety. It means, we become super-patriots. After this, slowly we try to enlarge this concept beyond the boundaries of our country because Mother Prithvi is not confined to our country alone. Thus, we become truly cosmopolitan. The concept that world is our family becomes true. Simultaneously, we learn not to waste our limited resources on trying to get unlimited material things, thinking that it will promote our happiness. This is not true. Experience is confirming it. Loving god Prithvi also meant to avoid polluting the Earth and the atmosphere. Today, science will not disagree with Rishis of Rig Veda.

Waters
(Varuna Devata)

Chapter 12

Varuna Devata (God of Waters)

A.A. Macdonell thinks that Varuna Devata is a Divya Devata (Heavenly). A reading of Rig Veda gives the confirmed view that Varuna is the Lord of all waters. These waters are found in the sky, on earth and under the earth. Then, one fails to understand how Varuna can be called a Divya Devata, i.e., heavenly.

A.A. Macdonell further says that efforts have been made to classify Devatas of Rig Veda on the basis of their relative importance. One category is of Devatas who are powerful. Indra Devata heads this category. But the other, equally important category, is of Devatas who are moralists. In this category Varuna heads the list. Therefore Varuna is not a popular god.[1]

---

[1]A.A. Macdonell, Vedic Mythology, Chaukhamba, Varanasi, 1984, p. 35.

A.A. Macdonell's view creates a confusion. A reading of Rig Veda makes it amply clear that both Varuna and Indra are connected with water. Varuna is an overall Lord of all waters—sky, earth and below the earth while Indra is a Lord only of rain water. Then why call Indra a great warrior and a powerful Lord and Varuna only a leader of moral gods? The author has tried to solve this riddle. He feels that Varuna is a natural phenomenon. So he is bound by the natural laws. He is, therefore, called a moralist. On the other hand, studies of Rig Veda[2] show that, to begin with, Indra was a man. Because of his continuous and excellent good deeds, he was raised to godhood. Efforts were made to make him a natural phenomenon. Several experiments were made and ultimately he was made the god of Rainfall and a natural god. In the past, as a man, Indra had fought innumerable wars. So, he has been painted as a powerful warrior god.

We find following Suktas and Mantras on Varuna Deva in Rig Veda:

	Sukta	*Rishi*	*God*
1.	1.17	Medhaatithi Kaandava	Indra, Varuna
2.	1.25	Shuneha Shepa Aajeegarti	Varuna
3.	1.137	Paruchepau Devodaasi	Mitra, Varuna
4.	1.152	Deerghatamaa Auchathya	Mitra, Varuna
5.	1.153	Deerghatamaa Auchathya	Mitra, Varuna
6.	2.28	Kurma Gratsamada, Gratsamada	Varuna

[2]Gupta, S.S., A Study of God Indra, Krishna Publishers, New Delhi, 2001.

7.	5.62	Shruta Vidaatreya	Mitra, Varuna
8.	5.63, 64	Archanaanaa Aatreya	Mitra, Varuna
9.	5.65, 66	Raat Havya Aatreya	Mitra, Varuna
10.	5.67, 68	Yajata Aatreya	Mitra, Varuna
11.	5.69, 70	Uroocha Kriraatreya	Mitra, Varuna
12.	5.71, 72	Vaahu Vrakta Aatreya	Mitra, Varuna
13.	6.67	Bharadwaajo Vaarhaspatya	Mitra, Varuna
14.	6.68	Bharadwaajo Vaarhaspatya	Indra, Varuna
15.	7.61	Vasishtha	Mitra, Varuna
16.	7.64	Vasishtha	Mitra, Varuna
17.	8.11	Suparna Kaandava	Indra, Varuna

Mantra

1.	1.15.6	Medhaatithi Kaandava	Mitra, Varuna
2.	1.23.4-6	Medhaatithi Kaandava	Mitra, Varuna
3.	1.24.6-15	Shuneha Shepa Aajeegarti	Varuna
4.	1.35.1	Hiranya Stoop Aangirasa	Agni, Mitra, Varuna, Raatri, Savita
5.	1.41.1-3, 7-9	Kandavo Ghaura	Mitra, Varuna
6.	1.43.3	Kandavo Ghaura	Mitra, Varuna, Rudra
7.	1.94.16	Kutsa Aangirasa	Mitra, Varuna
8.	1.136.1-5	Paruchepau Devodaasi	Mitra, Varuna
9.	1.139.2	Paruchepau Devodaasi	Mitra, Varuna
10.	1.151.2-9	Deerghatamaa Auchathya	Mitra, Varuna
11.	2.36.6	Gratsamada	Mitra, Varuna, Nabha
12.	2.41.4-6	Gratsamada	Mitra, Varuna
13.	3.62.1-3, 6-18	Vishwaamitra	Indra, Varuna
14.	4.42.7-10	Trasadasyu Paurookutsya	Indra, Varuna, Ashvino

15.	7.50.1	Vasishtha	Mitra, Varuna
16.	7.60.2-12	Vasishtha	Mitra, Varuna
17.	7.62.4-6	Vasishtha	Mitra, Varuna
18.	7.63.5, 6	Vasishtha	Mitra, Varuna
19.	7.66.1-3, 17-19	Vasishtha	Mitra, Varuna
20.	8.25.1-9, 13-24	Vishvamanaa Vaivashva	Mitra, Varuna
21.	8.42.1-3	Naabhaaka Kaandava, Archanaanaa Aatreya	Varuna
22.	8.69.11, 12	Priyamedha Aangirasa	Varuna
23.	8.101.1-5	Jamdagni Bhaargava	Mitra, Varuna
24.	10.132.2-7	Shakapooto Naarmedha	Mitra, Varuna

Out of all Rishis of Rig Veda only 25, i.e., 6.2% have pronounced their views on Varuna Devata. It is worthwhile to know why so few Rishis have offered their Mantras to Varuna and to which period do they belong. It will provide a correct place to Varuna Devata in the development of ideas.

A study of the above mentioned Suktas and Mantras on Varuna Devata, with the help of research methodology and information provided by science, helped the author to know the following facts about Varuna Devata.

WHO IS VARUNA DEVATA?

A reading of Rig Veda makes it amply clear that Varuna Devata is the overall Lord of all waters—water in the Sky, water on the Earth (oceans, rivers, tanks, pools, etc.) and water below the Earth. The following citations will prove it.

(i) "*Varuna is guardian of waters*" (Rishi Archanaanaa 5.63.1, Vasishtha 7.49.2, 7.64.1). These Rishis testify that Varuna is the Lord of all waters.

(ii) Rishi Vasishtha says that Varuna is the *Lord of Oceans* (7.87.6). Rishi Naabhaaka Kaandava confirms it (8.41.8).

(iii) *Varuna is the Lord of waters of seven rivers* (8.41.9). Rishi Priyamedha Aangirasa elaborates by saying that seven rivers keep pouring on the palate of Varuna (8.69.12). Rishi Vasishtha widens the scope by saying that Varuna is the powerful lord of rivers (7.64.2). Varuna sets free the water of the rivers (7.87.1). He, the thousand eyes, contemplates the waters of these rivers (7.34.10), the rivers flow by the power of Varuna (2.28.4). So, he is the lord of waters of rivers.

(iv) Several Rishis opine that Indra, *along with Mitra Devata, provokes Rains* (5.62.3, 5.63.3, 4, 5.68.2, 7.62.5, 7.64.4, 7.84.2).[3]

BIRTH OF VARUNA

It is essential to know the views of various Rishis about the birth of Varuna Devata.

Rishis say that Varuna is an Aaditya, i.e., a child of Mother Aditi (1.24.13, 2.41.6, 4.1.2, 7.60.5, 8.26.2, 3).

Mother Aditi is said to be a mother of several Aadityaas—Surya, Mitra, Usha, Savita, Bhaga etc. All

---

[3]While discussing god Mitra, an explanation has been given that Mitra, being a hot energy ray, evokes evaporation of water and this hot water air is converted, at a certain height, into clouds which cause rainfall.

of them are light, illuminating and scorcher. Naturally they derive these properties from Mother Aditi. It is worthwhile to know who this Mother Aditi is?

The studies of Rig Veda, with the help of science (as discussed earlier), convinced the author that Mother Aditi is the core part of the Sun whom science calls Photosphere. In this core part, continuous Nuclear Fusion is taking place with the result that there is a very high temperature—2×10^7 K to be precise and lot of gases.

Rishis establish a relationship between Surya Devata and Varuna Devata.

Rishi Vasishtha opines that Surya is friendly to Mitra and Varuna (7.60.3). Rishi Vasishtha further informs that Surya is the eyes of Mitra and Varuna (7.63.1).

The same view is conveyed in different ways by other Rishis.

Rishi Deerghatamaa Auchathya reveals that Varuna is born from Aakaasha (Heaven) and Prithvi (Earth) (1.151.3). This is a very important statement.

Thus, we have three views regarding the birth of Varuna Devata, viz., he is son of Mother Aditi, Surya is his eye and he is born from Aakaasha and Prithvi. In order to solve this riddle help of science was taken. Science reveals:

a. Atom is the smallest particle. Atoms make a molecule and molecules make a cell. This is the law of nature.

b. Some 500 crore years back, Young Sun was born. At that time, like today, it was a burning ball. In its central part, called core part or Photosphere, there were particles of various gases and metals. Due to their Nuclear Fusion tremendous heat was generated. It sent out waves of heat and light. In course of time, parts of this Young Sun broke. These parts are called Planetesimals. These Planetesimals were colliding with each other and combining also. In this way our *Earth was formed.*

Thus, Earth is daughter of the core part of the Sun. Earth, in the beginning, being a part of the Sun, was also like a ball and burning. It had also, like Sun, different gases and metal particles. With time, Earth started cooling down. The metal particles, being heavy, started accumulating at the central part of the Earth. So, they started driving out different gases from there.

Science tells us that the combination of a few gases like Oxygen and Hydrogen produces water. So, water was formed below the Earth and also on the Earth in the form of oceans.

This is the scientific explanation of how Varuna Devata was born.

It appears Rishis of Rig Veda, in their own way, were revealing this scientific truth when they said that Varuna Devata is the child of Mata Aditi (which is photosphere of the Sun), Surya is his eye and he is the Lord of all waters.

CHARACTERISTICS OF VARUNA

Rishis of Rig Veda have given the following characteristics of Varuna Devata:

1. *Varuna is a strict disciplinarian.* He punishes errors—Rishis pray: 'they commit errors' (1.25.1) but 'do not punish us' (1.25.2). Rishi Kurma Gratsamada confirms it (2.28.7).

2. *Varuna is kind-hearted also.* Rishi prays to free him from sins (1.24.15, 1.25.21). Rishi Vasishtha appeals: "whatever the offence which we men commit Varuna against divine beings, whatever law of thine we may through ignorance violate, do not you, divine Varuna, punish us on account of that inequity" (7.89.5).

3. *Varuna is "endowed with greatness, with wisdom, and with splendour, illumines the spacious* (Heaven and Earth)" (6.68.9).

4. *Varuna is knowledgeable.* He knows the path of the air and ocean (1.25.7). Varuna comes with undulating waters (1.161.14). Varuna even knows "the twelve months and their productions and that which supplementarily engendered" (1.25.8). It means Varuna knows the laws of Astronomy and accounting of time.

5. *Varuna is all pervading.* He abides in the three worlds (8.41.6). He "shines over Heaven and Earth, and all the world" (1.25.10).

6. Varuna is law observer—"He sat down amongst the (divine) progeny, to exercise supreme domination" (1.25.10). He enforces the divine laws (1.25.1, 1.151.3).

It will be worthwhile to know what are the natural laws of water. Science gives us some laws such as water flows from above towards below, water seeks its level, water, when boiled, becomes vapour and goes upward, towards the sky etc. Probably, the Rishis were pointing out these natural laws.

7. *Varuna helps in rainfall.* Rishi says: "Royal Mitra and Varuna, send down the rain" (5.62.3). Again, "Varuna has set free the water of the downward opening cloud for the (benefit of the) heaven, the earth, and the firmament; thence he is the monarch of all the worlds, watering the soil as the rain bedews the barley" (5.85.3, 5.85.4). Rishi prays Varuna to "stretch forth your arms for the prolongation of our existence, bedew with water the pastures of our cattle" (7.63.5, 7.84.2).

The question is: How Varuna Devata helps in rainfall? Science explains that heat causes evaporation of water and formation of clouds. These clouds, at a certain height, get condensed. The fall in temperature causes formation of dews. The wind helps in forming bigger dews which ultimately fall as rain.

Rishis also say the identical things when they talk of *Vaata Devata* (water evaporation), *Parjanya Devata* (clouds), *Maruta Devata* (winds) and *Indra Devata* (indicator of a zone—Troposphere).

ADVANTAGES FROM VARUNA

Rishis gave a list of advantages which men and animals get from Varuna. They are:

1. *Varuna causes rainfall* (5.68.5). Rains help in the growth of various vegetation. In other words wealth increases (4.41.8, 5.64.2, 70). This benefits men and animals.

2. Varuna causes rainfall and so *water level rises in rivers.* This helps in increase in agricultural yield and provides water to cows or cattle. This also increases yield of cows (5.62.3). It helps in liquidation of old and new debts (2.28.9).

3. *Varuna provides life as none can live without water.*

In the end, it can be said that Varuna Devata is a powerful Devata; it is one of the five basic elements, it provides life, it helps in vegetation, it helps animals and it enforces natural laws.

Vayu and Associate Deities

Chapter 13

Vayu Devata (Air)

Vayu Devata is one of the basic elements which has helped in the creation and subsistence of all the material things. Not only this. No life is possible without Vayu Devata.

We find the following Suktas and Mantras on Vayu Devata:

	Sukta	*Rishi*	*God*
1.	1.134	Paruchepau Devodaasi	Vayu
2.	4.48	Vaamdeva	Vayu
3.	10.168	Anilau Vaataayan	Vayu
4.	10.186	Ulo Vaataayan	

	Mantra		
1.	1.2.1-3	Madhuchandaa Vaishwaamitra	Vayu
2.	1.23.1	Medhaatithi Kaandava	Vayu
3.	1.135.1-3, 9	Paruchepau Devodaasi	Vayu

4.	2.41.1,2	Gratsamada	Vayu
5.	4.46.1	Vaamdeva	Vayu
6.	7.90.1-4	Vasishtha	Vayu
7.	7.91.1, 3	Vasishtha	Vayu
8.	7.92.1, 3-5	Vasishtha	Vayu
9.	8.26.20-25	Vishvamanaa Vaivashva	Vayu
10.	8.46.32	Vashau Ashva	Vayu
11.	8.101.9, 10	Nemo Bhaargava	Vayu
12.	1.2.4-6	Madhuchandaa Vaishwaamitra	Vayu, Indra
13.	1.23.2, 3	Medhaatithi Kaandava	Vayu, Indra
14.	1.35.4-8	Paruchepau Devodaasi	Vayu, Indra
15.	2.41.3	Gratsamada	Vayu, Indra
16.	4.46.2-7	Vaamdeva	Vayu, Indra
17.	7.90.5-7	Vasishtha	Vayu, Indra
18.	7.91.2, 4, 7	Vasishtha	Vayu, Indra
19.	7.92.2	Vasishtha	Vayu, Indra
20.	1.142.12	Deerghatamaa Auchathya	Swaha Kritya
21.	1.163.11	Deerghatamaa Auchathya	Ashva-Istuti
22.	4.17.12	Vaamdeva	Indra
23.	4.22.4	Vaamdeva	Indra
24.	4.38.4	Vaamdeva	Dadhikra
25.	5.83.4	Atri	Parjanya
26.	6.50.12	Rigishwaa Bhaaradwaja	Vishvedeva
27.	10.90.8, 13	Naaraayana	Purusha
28.	10.92.2, 13	Shaaryaata Maanav	Vishvedeva
29.	10.100.2	Duvasyurvaanandan	Vishvedeva

Out of all Rishis of Rig Veda, 4 Rishis have offered their complete Suktas to Vayu Devata, 8 Rishis have offered a few Mantras to Vayu Devata, 5 Rishis have offered their Mantras jointly to Vayu and Indra Devatas and 7 Rishis have only referred to Vayu Devata when they have offered their

Mantras to some other deity. This shows that Vayu is an important Devata but one fails to understand the rationale of the above pattern of offering Mantras to Vayu or only referring to Vayu.

Following ideas were found, or could be inferred from the above cited Suktas and Mantras.

ORIGIN OF VAYU DEVATA

Rishi Naaraayana reveals that Vayu was born from the breath of Viraat Purush (10.90.13).

Rishi Vasishtha informs that Aakaasha (Heaven) and Prithvi (Earth) bore Vayu (7.90.3).

The above views by themselves do not give a clear picture about the origin or birth of Vayu. So, help of science was sought.

The science tells that Vayu is nothing but a mixture of different gases. It mainly consists of oxygen, carbon dioxide and moisture. Science further says that when a part of the Sun broke and it became our Earth then it had lot of gases which it got from the Sun. Few gases gave us our air (Vayu).

When the views of Rishis were re-read in the light of the information provided by the science, both views appeared to be identical. Rishi Vasishtha says that Prithvi (Earth) bore Vayu and Rishi Naaraayana says that it is breath of Viraat Purush.

FORM OF VAYU

Rishi Anilau Vaataayan says that Vayu's form cannot be seen (10.168.4).

Rishi Vasishtha says that Vayu is white complexioned (7.91.3). When, according to one Rishi, Vayu cannot be seen then how its colour can be identified as white.

Rishi Vishvamanaa Vaivashva opines that Vayu is graceful (8.26.24).

Science says that Air (Vayu) cannot be seen. It is formless. It does not move. It is still. It has no colour.

It appears Rishis and science agree. White colour, as per science, is no colour. It is a mixture of colours. And then "graceful" can mean it does not move. It is calm and standstill.

AREA OF VAYU

Rishi Medhaatithi Kaandava invites Vayu from Aakaasha (Heaven) to drink Soma (1.23.2). It means the air is in Aakaasha also, an area beyond Antariksha (i.e., beyond 300 miles above our Earth).

The science seems to differ. According to science, air is upto 300 miles above earth. Thereafter, there is vacuum. Rishis call this 300 miles area Antariksha.

Some scholars should try to iron out this difference in these two views.

TYPES OF VAYU

Rishis of Rig Veda say that Vayu is of the following types:

1. **Marudagan Devata**

   They are also of two types:

   i) Hot air

   ii) Hot water vapours.

2. **Vaata Devata**
3. **Parjanya Devata**
4. **Apaam-Napaat Devata**

We will take up each type of Vayu, one after another.

ADVANTAGES FROM VAYU

Rishis have given, in their own way, the advantages which we get from Vayu. Some views are:

1. *Vayu is the soul* (10.168.4, 10.92.13). Rishi Ulo Vaataayan says it is a healing balm, it brings happiness, it prolongs our lives (10.186.1).

   Science accepts this view. No life is possible without air.

2. *Vayu is giver of corn, wealth (cattle) and male progeny.* Rishi Vasishtha prays Vayu to come and "bestow upon us enjoyable riches, bestow male progeny and wealth, comprehending cattle, and horses" (7.92.3). Rishi Vishvamanaa Vaivashva agrees (8.26.25). Probably here Rishis have failed to differentiate between Vayu and Vaata Devata.

   These Rishis seem to establish a relationship between Vayu and Rains. Science admits that there is a relationship between the two but it is not that direct one as Rishis seem to think. It is through Vaata Devata.

VAYU AND SOMA

Rishis invite Vayu Devata to come and enjoy delicious Soma which they have prepared. They seem to think that it will please the mighty Vayu and help them in getting health, wealth, cattle, male progeny and valuable rains.

Chapter 14

Devata Marudagan (Wind)

A.A. Macdonell opines that amongst the Devatas of Rig Veda Marudagan occupies an important place. They are a group of Devatas.[1]

The following material is found in Rig Veda on Marudagan:

	Sukta	*Rishi*	*God*
1.	1.37, 1.38, 1.39	Kaandava Ghaura	Marut
2.	1.85, 1.86, 1.87, 1.88	Gautama Raahugana	Marut
3.	1.64	Naudhaa Gautama	Marut
4.	1.68		
5.	1.166, 1.168	Agastya	Marut

[1]A.A. Macdonell, Vedic Mythology (in Hindi), Chaukhamba Vidya Bhawan, Varanasi, 1984, p. 147.

6.	2.34	Gratsamada Bhaargava Shaunak	Marut
7.	5.87	Aivyaamrudraatreya	Marut
8.	5.52, 5.53, 5.54, 5.55, 5.56, 5.57, 5.58, 5.59, 5.60	Shyaavaashva Aatreya	Marut
9.	6.66	Bharadwaajo Vaarhaspatya	Marut
10.	7.56, 7.57, 7.58	Vasishtha	Marut
11.	8.7	Punarvatsa Kaandava	Marut
12.	8.91	Poota Daksha Aangirasa	Marut
13.	8.20	Saubhari Kaandava	Marut
14.	10.77, 10.78	Syumarishimir Bhaargava	Marut

Mantras

1.	1.167.2-11, 1.171.1.2	Agastya	Marut
2.	1.6.4, 6, 8, 9	Madhuchandaa Vaishwaamitra	Marut
3.	1.15.2	Medhaatithi Kaandava	Marut
4.	2.30.11	Gratsamada	Marut
5.	8.96.11	Tirashchee Aangirasa	Marut
6.	7.59.1-11, 7.101.18	Vasishtha	Marut
7.	3.26, 4-6	Vishwaamitra	Marut
8.	5.61, 11-16	Shyaavaashva Aatreya	Marut
9.	6.48, 11-15	Shanyurvaarhaspatya	Marut

Out of all Rishis of Rig Veda 18 Rishis, i.e., 4.5% have studied Marut Devata and expressed their views. It is quite a good number when compared with other Devatas.

Unfortunately, these Rishis have not been arranged in a chronological order and so it is difficult to be definite on the development of ideas on Marut Devata.

WHO ARE MARUTS?

Rishi Gautama Raahugana reveals that Maruts are the sons of Prithvi (Earth) (1.85.3).

Rishi Kaandava Ghaura opines that Maruts are the sons of Rudra (1.38.7, 1.39.4).

Rishi Kaandava Ghaura further reveals that Maruts are the sons of Aakaasha (Sky). Another Rishi confirms it (10.77.2).

Thus, Maruts are the children of Prithvi and Aakaasha.

Rishis have said that Prithvi (Earth) and Aakaasha (Sky) bore Vayu (7.90.3). A Rishi also expressed the view that Vayu was born from the breath of Viraat Purush (10.90.13).

It can, therefore, be concluded that Vayu and Marut are almost the same. They have almost the same parentage.

Marudagan, Rishis tell, reside in Antariksha (firmament) (1.6.4). They also abide in the upper, the middle, or the lower heaven (5.60.6), i.e., Aakaasha or Heaven. This statement is not confirmed by science.

Rishi Shyaavaashva Aatreya says that Maruts are universal (5.58.3).

Rishis of Rig Veda, in their own way, have said that Vayu is in Aakaasha (Sky or Heaven).

Science tells us that Air (Vayu) is upto 300 miles above earth. Thereafter, there is vacuum. Rishis call this 300 miles area Antariksha.

So, it appears that Rishis think that Vayu and Maruts, both, are in Antariksha (upto 300 miles above Earth) and also in Aakaasha (Heaven). But science differs. It says that above Antariksha, in Aakaasha, there is vacuum. So, it appears that Rishis were not very clear about the area of operation of both Vayu and Maruts. But one thing is clear. Their area of operation upto Antariksha is identical.

DIFFERENCE BETWEEN VAYU AND MARUTS

It appears Rishis were not clear about the difference between Vayu and Maruts. For example, Rishis say that Vayu flows (1.134.1, 2.41.1, 4.48.5, 7.92.5, 8.26.20). A Rishi adds "Vayu, his voice spread thundering around, he moves along sweeping the sky, tinting purple (the quarters of the horizons), he advances, raising the dust of the earth" (10.168.1).

Rishis also opine "Marut is self moving deer-borne" (1.87.4). Again, like birds they fly to the end of firmament (Antariksha) (5.59.7). They come from heaven (Aakaasha) (1.38.2). They move with such speed as to make all things tremble (1.39.1, 2, 1.85.4, 1.87.1, 1.167.4, 5.59.3).

So, it appears, according to Rishis, Vayu and Maruts, both, flow, sometimes slowly and at other times with vigour and forcibly.

Science seems to differ. Science thinks that Air does not move. It has enveloped the Earth upto 300 miles. But when due to heat or Agni, some columns of air get heated, they become lighter and move upward. The space which they vacate is filled in by the near about air. Thus, air starts moving. Science calls this moving air wind (Marudagan).

It can, therefore, be concluded that though Rishis were not very clear in their mind about the difference between Vayu and Maruts, but the later Rishis could clearly differentiate between Vayu and Marudagan when they said that when Vayu moves, it is called Maruts (wind) or Marudagan.

Rishi Paruchepau Devodaasi reveals that Vayu "beget the Maruts" (1.134.4). He explains the difference between the two but is not very clear.

NUMBER OF MARUTS

Rishis differentiate between Marut and Marudagan, one is singular and the other is plural. So, naturally the question arises: How many are the Maruts or Marudagan?

Rishi Shyaavaashva Aatreya reveals "May the seven times seven all potent (Maruts, aggregated as) as a single troop...." (5.52.17). Thus, there are 49 varieties of Maruts. It appears Rishi is saying that there are seven main vertical columns and each main vertical column has seven sub-columns, thus making the total number of 49. All of them constitute Marudagan. No further details are found about these 49 Maruts.

Help of science was sought. Science says that Air and Wind are found upto 300 miles above the earth. Science divides this 300 miles zone into four vertical zones:

1. *Troposphere*—It goes upto 10 miles above earth. It is very active zone.
2. *Stratosphere*—It goes from 10 miles to 30 miles above earth. It is a quieter zone. Aeroplanes fly in this area.
3. *Mesosphere*—It is spread out from 30 miles to 50 miles above earth. It is quite cold.
4. *Thermosphere*—It goes from 50 miles to 300 miles above the earth.

Science tells us that as we go up, towards the sky, the area gets more and more cool with the result that weight and density of the Air (Vayu) or Wind (Maruts) goes on decreasing. Thus, science thinks that there are four types of winds (Maruts) vertically. It does not further sub-divide wind of each zone vertically, which the wise Rishis seem to do.

One the other hand ancient Rishis thought that there are main seven types of zones vertically and then each type of zone has seven sub-types, making the number 49. However, details are wanting. It is for the scientists to let us know the truth.

Rishis opine that all the types of Maruts were born at the same time, "who are of one age, one residence, one divinity..." (1.165.1). "None of them are older, none younger...none hold a middle rank..." (5.59.6). "They are brothers, of whom no one is elder, no one the younger..." (5.60.5).

The Rishis do not elaborate the above point.

Thus, it can be said that when Rishis of Rig Veda gave us seven zones of air in which Marudagans move and further sub-divided each of these seven zones in seven sub-zones, thus making 49 zones in which 49 types of Marudagans move, then science gave us only four zones in which wind (Marudagan) moves. Obviously, Rishis, it appears, made more detailed study and therefore made 49 zones.

One should try to guess the basis on which Rishis divided this area of wind into 49 zones.

Science tells us that due to several types of heat—the heat of the Sun which comes to earth through seven colour energy waves of different temperature, heat of the earth coming from below the earth, heat on the surface of the earth created by fire etc.—the air on the earth and above it, gets heated up. Heated air gets expanded and becomes thinner. This thinner air naturally starts rising upward. To fill in the space vacated by this thin air, the surrounding denser air moves in. Movement of air starts. Thus, god Marudagan (wind) are formed. Science calls them wind.

Science further tells us that the heat thus generated on the surface of the earth, which gives heat to the contracting air, is not uniform all over.

It is a known fact that the temperature is maximum at the equator and lowest at the North and South poles. Thus, it can be guessed that the displacement of the air on getting heated up is not uniform all over the surface of the earth. So, it rises upto different heights as per the thinness or lightness caused due to different degrees of heats. It is possible that Rishis might have classified Marudagan as per their capacity to go up.

Science also talks of water vapours. It tells us that due to heat of the Sun in the form of various rays (Mitra, Usha, Savita, Bhag, etc.), heat that comes from the inner part of the earth and other heats generated on the surface of the earth (Fire, etc.) water of the surface of the earth continuously evaporates. It is probably due to this evaporation of water that in spite of the continuous flow of rivers water in the oceans, they never overflow. The evaporated water, in the form of vapours, is lighter than the atmospheric pressure and so it rises. At a certain height it takes the form of clouds. This water vapour, while moving upward, also vacates some air space and the surrounding air, to fill in this space, rushes towards it. It also produces Marudagans (winds).

Science tells us that the water vapours, which take the form of clouds, are of various types. Like Howard, a London Pharmacist, in 1803, named the three basic groups. Today clouds are classified in ten types.

We can therefore infer that:

i) Various types of Marudagans are formed when the dry air of different places is heated up and goes up. As the heat is uniform at all places on our earth, so the heated air's capacity to go up in the atmosphere is also not the same. It rises to different heights. It is one cause to form different types of Marudagan.

ii) Marudagan are also formed when the water evaporates due to the various types of heat. It is different from the dry heated air. Science has already found out their ten types.

It appears, thousands of years back, Rishis of Rig Veda discovered many more factors and on the basis of these factors classified the moving air, i.e., wind (Marudagan) into 49 types.

Thus, it can be concluded that Rishis of Rig Veda were very knowledgeable persons and they could find out the secrets of the nature which science is able to reveal today.

SOME UNANSWERED QUESTIONS

There are some questions which need explanation. For example:

1. Rishi Agastya says that Marudagan scatter the dense vapour, i.e., cloud and the result is rainfall. This does not seem to be a scientific truth. Marudagan help in joining the small tiny drops of water and therefore rain falls. If it will scatter the clouds, there will be no rain.

2. Rishi Shyaavaashva Aatreya reveals that red steeds are yoked in the car of Marudagan (5.6.6, 5.57.4).

One is unable to understand it. Why red steed, what do they denote?

Some scholars should solve this riddle.

Chapter 15

Vaata Devata (Vapours)

A reading of Rig Veda shows that very few Rishis have expressed their views on Vaata Devata and most of them, at places, have not been able to differentiate between Vayu Devata, Parjanya Devata, Marudagan and Vaata Devata. The reason seems to be that Vaata Devata, Marudagan and Parjanya Devatas—all are a part of Vayu Devata, and probably these Rishis were in the beginning stage of the studies of Vaata Devata.

The following Suktas and Mantras are found on Vaata Devata:[1]

	Sukta	*Rishi*	*God*
1.	10.168	Anilo Vaataayan	Vayu
2.	10.186	Ulo Vaataayan	Vayu

[1]As per A.A. Macdonell, Dr. Surya Kanta and my own readings.

Mantra			
1.	1.28.6	Shuneha Shepa Aajeegarti	Ulookhalam
2.	1.134.3	Paruchepau Devodaasi	Vayu
3.	2.1.6	Gratsamada Bhaargava Shaunak	Agni
4.	2.14.3	Gratsamada	Agni
5.	4.17.12	Vaamdeva	Indra
6.	5.41.3	Atri	Vishvedeva
7.	6.50.12	Rijishwaa Bhaaradwaja	Vishvedeva
8.	9.97.52	Kutsa	Pavamaan Soma
9.	10.92.13	Shaaryaata Maanaava	Vishvedeva

To have a better understanding of Vaata Devata, it will be better to study Suktas 10.168 and 10.186 in entirety and then proceed further.

Sukta 10.168

This Sukta has been offered to Vayu Devata. A reading of the Sukta shows that Rishi Anilo Vaataayan has used the word Vaata (not Vayu) in the verses. Verses of the Sukta are as below.

10.168.1

"(I proclaim) the greatness of the impetuous Vayu (read Vaata), his voice spread thundering around, he moves along sweeping the sky, tinting purple (the quarters of the horizon), he advances, raising the dust of the earth."

This means the Vaata moves with speed, vigour and great noise.

10.168.2

"Solid masses advance to meet the wind; the mares come to him as to battle; associated with them and in the same car the divinity proceeds, the sovereign of all this world."

This also shows the speed and velocity of Vaata Devata.

10.168.3

"Traversing the firmament by its path (Vayu—read Vaata), rests not for a single day; the friends of waters, the first born, the utterer of truth—where has he been generated, whence was he manifested."

This verse reveals many important things about Vaata. First, it limits its scope upto firmament, i.e., Antariksha and secondly, it has a close relationship with water.

10.168.4

"The soul of gods, the germ of the world, this divinity moves according to his pleasure; his voice are heard, his form is not (seen), let us worship that Vaata with oblations."

Vaata has no form, it cannot be seen but its presence is felt by the sound that it makes.

Thus, this Sukta gives some characteristics of Vaata Devata, viz., it is formless, it cannot be seen, it moves with vigour, velocity and sound, its range is within Antariksha (i.e., upto 300 miles above earth) and it has a close relationship with water.

Now let us study the other important Sukta—10.186.

Sukta 10.186

10.186.1

"May Vaata breathe into our hearts a healing balm, bringing happiness; may he prolong our lives."

Vaata cures diseases, prolongs life and brings happiness.

10.186.2

"You, Vaata, are both our father and our brother and our friend; cause us to live."

Vaata is close to us. It helps us in being healthy and live a long life.

10.186.3

"That store of ambrosia, Vaata, which is placed in your house, give us of it that we may live."

Vaata is a store of ambrosia and so is health giver and longevity giver.

In this Sukta other characteristics of Vaata have been given, viz., Vaata is a curer of diseases, a health giver and a storehouse of nectar.

These two Suktas are important but they do not give a definite idea who Vaata is? How has it originated? And how he performs the above functions?

Let us turn to some other Mantras and see whether they provide a clearer picture.

1.28.6

This Mantra does not add to the knowledge, because it talks of preparing Soma juice. But indirectly it establishes a relationship between wind and vegetation.

1.134.3

This Mantra simply says that Vayu yokes two horses, i.e., it moves and lights up the dawn.

2.1.6

This Mantra mainly concerns Agni Devata but shows that Agni is strength of Maruts who move about.

2.14.6

It shows wind causes the rainfall.

4.17.12

It says that "wind is driven by thundering clouds." Thus, it again establishes a relationship between wind and rainfall. And since Indra is the god of Rainfall, he come in.

5.41.3

In this Mantra the speed of Vishvedeva is compared with the swiftness of the wind.

6.50.12

Rishi prays that may Vayu along with other deities make us happy, sending rain and Vaata grant us abundant food.

9.97.12

It does not add to the knowledge.

10.92.13

Vayu is the friend of Vishvedeva, the grandson of the waters, which is the soul of all.

The above Mantras do not give a clear picture about Vaata Devata except giving broad hints. These hints are:

1. Vaata is related to Vayu (Air).
2. Vaata is related to Marudagan (Wind).
3. Vaata is connected with water, with the thundering clouds which Rishis call Parjanya and with Indra, i.e., God of Rainfall. All this establishes a relationship of Vaata with water (in different forms) and vegetation.
4. Vaata moves with vigour and speed and creates a roaring sound.
5. Vaata's area of activity is confined to firmament or Antariksha—i.e. upto 300 miles above earth. There is no air beyond it. There is vacuum which is called Aakaasha or Sky, or Heaven.

   Science, on the other hand, limits the area of activity of Vaata to only upto ten miles above the earth, i.e., upto the end of Troposphere.
6. Vaata cannot be seen. It has no form. It can only be felt.
7. Vaata is like a healing balm. It purifies. It gives happiness. It gives health and longevity.

   In spite of these characteristics, the author could not identify Vaata Devata in the modern terminology. So, help of science was taken.

Science says:

1. Air is composed of gases. The main gases are oxygen, carbon-dioxide and water.

2. Air, by itself, is still. It does not move.

3. Air is upto 300 miles above earth called firmament or Antariksha. Beyond it, is vacuum.

4. The heat of the Sun, the Fire on the earth, specially forest fire (Davaagni) and the Fire below the earth (Badvaagni or Badvaanala) heats the air. Thus, air gets heated in two ways.

   (a) Air is heated where there is no water such as deserts.

   (b) Air is heated where there is water such as oceans, rivers etc. Here the heat generates water-vapours.

   In both cases, the heated air becomes thinner and lighter and so moves towards the sky.

   The water-vapour moves with a force. It has speed.

5. As the heated air (both types) moves upward, a vacuum is created. To fill in this vacuum the adjoining air rushes towards it. Science calls the moving air wind. Rishis call it Marudagan.

   As the water-vapours rise in the atmosphere, it starts cooling. Ultimately it takes the form of clouds which Rishis called Parjanya.

6. At a certain height these water-vapours or clouds become so much condensed that water-vapours are re- converted into tiny drops of water or dews. These dews or tiny water drops sit on the particles of sand,

carbon, dust particles etc. floating in the wind, i.e., Marudagan.

7. Because of wind, i.e., Marudagan, the tiny water drops combine and become bigger and heavier. Ultimately they fall in the form of Rain.
8. Rain helps vegetation. Rain drops are caused from water-vapours. These vapours, due to heat, remove all impurities of water and so this water is pure, health giver and happiness giver.

The description of science, when compared with the views of Rishis, then the following conclusions can be made:

Air	=	Vayu
Wind	=	Marudagan
Clouds	=	Parjanya
Firmaments, i.e., area upto a height of 300 miles above Earth	=	Antariksha

Troposphere = Where water vapours get cooled and converted into tiny dews of water drops is *Indra-Loka*

In this way, the only factor left is water-vapours. It should be, in the term of Rishis, Vaata Devata.

Seeing Vaata Devata as Water-Vapour, we find all the characteristics of Vaata Devata given by Rishis are the same as given by Science. Both are one and the same.

Chapter 16

Parjanya Devata (The Clouds)

A.A. Macdonell opines that amongst the Devatas of Rig Veda, Parjanya Devata is the most secondary deity. Very few Rishis have pronounced their views on him and consequently only three Suktas and less than thirty Mantras have been offered to him. Parjanya denotes the "Rain clouds".[1]

In Rig Veda following Suktas and Mantras refer to Parjanya Devata:

	Sukta	*Rishi*	*God*
1.	5.83	Atri	Parjanya
2.	7.101	Kumar Aagney, Vasishtha	Parjanya
3.	7.102	Kumar Aagney, Vasishtha	Parjanya

[1]A.A. Macdonell, Vedic Mythology (Hindi), Chaukhamba Vidya Bhawan, Varanasi, 1984, p. 157.

Mantras

1.	5.42.14	Atri	Vishvedeva
2.	5.63.3-6	Archanaanaa Aatreya	Mitra, Varuna
3.	8.91.5	Apaalaa Aatreyee	Indra
4.	9.22.2	Asti Kaashyap, Deval Kaashyap	Pavamaana Soma
5.	6.49.6	Rigishwaa Bhaaradwaaja	Vishvedeva
6.	6.50.12	Rigishwaa Bhaaradwaaja	Vishvedeva
7.	6.52.6-16	Rigishwaa Bhaaradwaaja	Vishvedeva
8.	1.39.9	Kandava Ghaura	Marudagan
9.	9.113.3	Kashyapa Maareecha	Pavamaana Soma
10.	1.164.51	Deerghatamaa Auchathya	Surya, Parjanya, Agni
11.	10.98.1-8	Devaapi Aarishtishema	Deva Gana
12.	3.55.17-2	Prajaapatir Vaarchya	Vishvedeva
13.	9.2.9	Medhaatithi Kaandava	Pavamaana Soma
14.	7.10.3	Vasishtha	Mandooka
15.	8.6.1	Vatsa Kaandava	Indra
16.	9.82.3	Vasurbhaaradwaaja	Pavamaana Soma
17.	10.66.10	Vasukrana Vaasukra	Vishvedeva
18.	5.53.6	Shyaavaashva Aatreya	Marudagan

Out of all Rishis of Rig Veda only 17, i.e., 4.2% have given their views on Parjanya Devata. This confirms the view of A.A. Macdonell.

So far we have not arranged these Rishis in a chronological order. So, it is not possible to find out authentically the development of the ideas on Parjanya Devata.

WHO IS PARJANYA DEVATA?

Rishi Rigishwaa Bhaaradwaaja says "Parjanya and Vaata, showerers of rain" (6.49.6) and "May Rudra.... sending rain....and may Parjanya and Vaata grant us abundant food" (6.50.12).

Thus, Rishi Bhaaradwaaja thinks that Parjanya and Vaata are two distinct deities and both combined cause rain.

Science agrees with this view. Water-vapour is Vaata Devata. This Vaata is warm and so gets lighter. It goes towards the sky. As it ascends, it gets cooler because the temperature goes on becoming cooler. At one particular area, it gets quite condensed and water-vapours start re-converting into tiny dews. These dews mount on the particles of sand, carbon, dust, etc. floating in the air. In this condensed shape the water-vapour, i.e. Vaata Devata becomes cloud, i.e., Parjanya.

Rishi Vasishtha Maitraavaruni observes "one form of Parjanya is like a barren cow the other produces offsprings" (7.101.3). Again, "...preceded by light, which milk the water yielding udder; for he, the showerer, (thereby) becoming quickly manifest, loudly roars, engendering the (lightning) infant, the embryo of the plants" (7.101.1).

Science tells us that Agni of Surya, other Agnis on earth and Agni below the earth heat the Vayu (Air). The warm air of the deserts and other places, where there is no water, gets lighter and moves towards the sky. Similarly, the warm air of the places where there is water, takes with it water-vapours which also go towards the sky. Both, at a certain height, get condensed and become cloud. Parjanya (clouds) without water have been compared with a barren cow and clouds with water, with milk yielding cow. Rishi was giving a scientific truth.

These clouds loudly roar and lightning takes place.

RELATION WITH INDRA DEVATA

Rishi Vatsa Kaandava establishes a relationship of Indra and Parjanya. He observes "Indra, who is great in might like Parjanya the distributor of rain..." (8.6.1). Again, "when his (Indra's) wrath thundered, dividing Vratra joint by joint, then he drove the waters to the ocean" (8.6.13). "You, Indra, have cast into the rushing streams him who lay obstructing your copious waters" (8.6.16).

Thus, a relationship of Parjanya (rain cloud) and Indra has been established and Rishi says that Indra's active help causes rain.

Science tells that Vaata Devata, which is water-vapours, goes up and due to cooler atmosphere, starts getting cooler. The area upto 10 miles above the earth is called Troposphere. It is here that water-vapours get sufficiently condensed and are re-converted into tiny drops of water. These drops mount particles which are floating in the air. The weight and size of the tiny water dews is so small that they float but do not fall in form of rain.

The author feels that wise Rishis of Rig Veda have called the area of Troposphere as Indra Loka.

So Indra gets associated with rain and also, Parjanya, the clouds.

RELATION OF INDRA, MARUDAGAN AND PARJANYA

Rishi Shyaavaashva Aatreya establishes a relationship of Marudagan with rainfall. He says "Leaders (of the rain), munificent givers, they cause that which is the treasury (of water) to fall from the sky for (the benefit of) the donor (of the offering); they let loose the rain cloud, and the shedders of rain spread (everywhere) with (abundant) water" (5.53.6).

Rishi Prajaapatirvaachya establishes a relationship amongst Parjanya, Indra and Marudagan. He says:

"When the showerer roars in other (regions) he sends down the rain upon a different herd, for he is the victor, the auspicious, the sovereign; great and unequalled is the might of gods" (3.55.17).

"Our king, the nourisher of all, abides (in the firmament) nearest to this earth like a benevolent friend; the valiant (Maruts) precede him (when abroad), and dwell on his mansion; great and unequalled in might of gods" (3.55.21).

"The plants, Indra, come to perfection by you from you the waters (flow); earth bears her treasurers for you; may we, your friends, be sharers of these blessings; great and unequalled is the might of Gods" (3.55.22).

Rishi Deerghatamaa Auchathya says: "The uniform water passes upwards and downwards in the course of days; clouds give joy to the earth, fires rejoice the heaven" (1.164.51).

Rishi Kaandavo Ghaura prays: "...come to us, Maruts with undivided protective assistance, as the lightning (bring) the rain" (1.39.9). Further, "you have harnessed the spotted dear to your chariot..." (1.39.6).

Rishi Atri says: "Send down for us, Maruts, the rain from heaven; drops of the rainy charge descend; come down Parjanya, sprinkling water by this thundering (cloud), you who are the sender of rain, our protector" (5.83.6).

Rishi Vasukarna Vaasukra, in his own style, gives the relationship:

"We offer praise to the company of the Maruts ...who, encouraged by Indra, and instructed by Varuna, have acquired a portion of the light of the Sun, the wise worshippers beget the sacrifice" (10.66.2).

"...may Parjanya be the showerer (of rain)..." (10.6.6).

"May...Vaata and Parjanya, (the utterers) of the mighty thunder, the waters, the plants, amplify our praise..." (10.66.10).

These Rishis, in their own style, have tried to establish a relationship between Parjanya, Indra and Marudagan. They have tried to explain that rainfall is possible only when these three combine.

Let us see what science has to say.

Science tells us that water-vapours, at the height of Troposphere (upto 10 miles above earth) (which the author thinks is Indra Loka), get condensed due to Indra Devata. The water-vapours are reconverted into tiny water drops which mount particles floating in the air. These droplets are too small and so cannot fall on earth in the form of rain. The wind, which Rishis call Marudagan, helps these tiny water drops to combine and form bigger and heavier water drops. Then rain starts falling.

The Rishis seem to be saying the same thing.

Indra Loka helps in conversion of water-vapours into tiny water drops. And it is the winds (Marudagan) which take clouds, i.e., Parjanya from place to place—horizontally and vertically. Thus, helping in the formation of bigger drops. Rishi Kaandavo Ghaura's "harnessed the spotted deer" are nothing but drops of water.

ADVANTAGES FROM PARJANYA DEVATA

1. Rishi Atri says that "Parjanya fertilizes the soil with showers" and thus earth becomes fit for growing vegetation (5.83.4, 5, 10).

2. Parjanya waters the plants (10.66.10). This increases agricultural produce which is helpful to men and animals.

   "Parjanya, the sender of rain, may he be pleased (to grant) us food" (7.102.1).

3. The rainfall waters the rivers and fields which provide "abundant beverage for the kine" (5.83.80). Thus, the cows benefit.

4. Parjanya " is the cause of the impregnation of plants,

of cows, of mares, of women" (7.102.2). Thus, in the period of Rig Veda, due to Parjanya vegetation, animlas and human population increased. This was good.

5. "The frogs...utter aloud praises agreeable to Parjanya" (7.103.1). This is a time of rejoining for frogs and their mating (7.103.2-6). One wonders why Rishis have stressed this advantage so much.

Chapter 17

Apaam-Napaat Devata (Lightning in the Sky)

Apaam-Napaat Devata, it appears, has not been a popular Devata with the Rishis of Rig Veda. Only two Suktas have been offered to him and hardly thirty times he has been referred to in Mantras. The details are given below:

	Sukta	*Rishi*	*God*
1.	2.35	Gratsamada	Apaam-Napaat
2.	10.30	Kavasha Ailuha	Apaam-Napaat
	Mantras		
1.	1.70.3	Paraashar Shaakatya	Agni
2.	1.143.1	Deerghatamaa Auchathya	Agni
3.	1.186.5	Agastya	Vishvedeva
4.	2.31.6	Gratsamada	Vishvedeva
5.	3.1.13	Vishwaamitra	Agni
6.	3.5.3	Vishwaamitra	Agni

7.	3.9.1	Vishwaamitra	Agni
8.	6.50.13	Rigishwaa Bhaaradwaaja	Vishvedeva
9.	7.9.3	Vasishtha	Agni
10.	7.35.13	Vasishtha	Vishvedeva
11.	8.43.9	Viroop Aangirasa	Agni
12.	10.45.1-3	Vatsdri	Agni

Only two Suktas have been offered to Apaam-Napaat and only twelve Mantras have been offered to him. Even in these Mantras in which his reference has come, the devata is Agni (8 times) and Vishvedeva (4 times). One must try to find out the reasons for it and the relationship of Apaam-Napaat with these two deities.

FEATURES OF APAAM-NAPAAT

A reading of Rig Veda, specially the above Suktas and Mantras, gives the following important ideas about Apaam-Napaat Devata:

1. Sukta 2.35 gives the clear indication that Apaam-Napaat is Agni in the sky.

   Rig Veda talks of two types of Agni in the sky:

   (a) Agni in the Sun (Surya) due to Nuclear Fusion. It gives light and heat to Surya Devata.

   (b) Agni in the sky, i.e., Apaam-Napaat. A Rishi says that Agni was first born in the sky (10.45.1). It resides as lightning in Parjanya (10.45.3).

2. *Apaam-Napaat is the grandson of waters* (2.35.1, 2.35.9, 3.9.1). One will like to know how is he the grandson of waters.

3. "The pure water are gathered round the pure and brilliant grandson of the waters" (2.35.3), i.e., Apaam-Napaat.
4. Apaam-Napaat shines amidst the waters with pure and divine (radiance) (2.35.8).
5. Apaam-Napaat has generated himself as an embryo in these (waters) (2.35.13).
6. Apaam-Napaat has "a golden form, of golden aspect, of golden hue, and (shines) seated upon a seat of gold" (3.35.10.11).
7. Apaam-Napaat shines "with imperishable rays" (3.35.14).
8. Apaam-Napaat moves tortuously in the clouds (2.35.9).
9. Apaam-Napaat is "sounding and swift moving grandson of waters" (2.35.1).
10. Apaam-Napaat is arrayed in lightning (2.35.9).

All these features of Apaam-Napaat give some ideas about him, such as:

(a) Apaam-Napaat is the grandson of waters and is connected with Parjanya. It is clear that Parjanya is born out of waters and Apaam-Napaat is born of Parjanya. Hence he is called the grandson of waters.

(b) He is Agni of the sky connected with Parjanya and not the Sun's Agni.

(c) He is golden in colour, has radiance and imperishable rays and arrayed in lightning.

(d) He moves tortuously, i.e., not in a straight line.

Yet, these ideas do not help us in identifying Apaam-Napaat in a definite way. So, let us take the help of science.

Science tells us that water clouds have electric charges. One is the positive charge and the other is the negative charge. Sometimes, due to water these charges of cloud get connected and therefore there is lightning. This lightning moves in a zigzag way and sometimes falls on the earth also. It is accompanied by a thunder.

The above description given by Rishis and the explanation given by the science are identical. So, Apaam-Napaat is nothing but lightning of the sky.

ADVANTAGES OF APAAM-NAPAAT

1. Since Apaam-Napaat is the grandson of waters and connected with waters (Parjanya), therefore, Rishis pray him to give food (2.35.1).

   The Rishis reveal that Apaam-Napaat produces shrubs (2.35.8). The rivers flow with water because of him (2.35.9).

2. Rishi Agastya prays that lightning may grant us happiness (1.186.5).

   It appears that Rishis think that there is some relationship between lightning and rainfall.

A FEW UNANSWERED QUESTIONS

It is necessary that scholars should search out answers of the following questions:

1. How the three Divine Females (Ila, Saraswati and Bharati) are specially connected with Apaam-Napaat (2.35.5)?
2. How Ahirbudhnya, Ajaekapaad, Trita, Qbhukshin, and Savita are associated with Apaam-Napaat?
3. What is the relationship of Agni and Vishvedeva with Apaam-Napaat?

The above discussion shows that Apaam-Napaat is closely associated with Vayu and water. So, if we observe the natural laws of Vayu and water, work in their cooperation and do not try to exploit and pollute them beyond a reasonable limit we will get benefits from them. Man will be happy and healthy.

BOOK II

Spiritual Gods

Chapter 18

Pitra Devata

Rishis of Rig Veda observed that in spite of the availability of basic five elements—Sky, Earth, Agni, Water and Air, all the living beings die after an interval of time. They tried to search the causes of death. They discovered that to keep the living beings alive, another element, which they called SOUL ENERGY, is needed (see Appendix II—Importance of Shradha of this chapter).

Several Rishis of Rig Veda gave ideas on Pitra Devata. The list of their Suktas and Mantras has been given in Appendix I.

It appears Rishis, sometimes, do not give a straight answer to a question. It becomes, therefore, necessary to use logic and sometimes conjecture to find out an answer. This method, whenever necessary, has been employed.

I. WHO IS PITRA?

Rishi Yaamaayan says "Let this our adoration be

today addressed to those Pitras, our predecessors, to those our successors, who have departed (to the world of the manes); to these who are seated in the terrestrial sphere..." (10.15.2).

According to Sayana, Purvaasah means an elder brother, father, grandfather and the like, born before the birth of the worshipper; '*Uparaasah*' means younger brother, sons, etc.

Thus, all the dead, who are close relation to us, become Pitra.

Here several questions arise:

(i) **Why Sayana limits elders upto grandfather? Why not beyond them?**

Here, to get an answer, the method of logic and conjecture has been employed.

Rishis of Rig Veda reveal that our Pitras, after an interval of time, take rebirth. When a Pitra takes rebirth, he ceases to be a Pitra.

In the time of Rig Veda, the span of life was long. So, it can be said that by the time of birth of a grandson, the time-interval becomes quite long and normally, by that time, the soul of great-grandfather takes re-birth. So, it was said that normally Pitras are upto grandfather.

(ii) **After death, who becomes a Pitra?**

A reading of Rig Veda makes it evidently clear that the combination and permutation of the five basic or principal elements—Sky, Earth, Fire, Air and Water go to make all the material things including the human body. Science agrees.

Rishis reveal that besides the body there is a soul which primarily is responsible for giving the material bodies, including human body, life. This soul never dies. For example:

(a) Rishis Bandhu, Subandhu, Shrut Bandhu, Vipra Bandhu etc. reveal: "Although your spirit have gone far away to Yama...we bring back that (spirit) of your..." (10.58.1).

(b) They further reveal: "Although your spirit have gone far away to heaven we bring back that (Spirit) of your..." (10.58.2).

(c) "Although your spirit have gone far away to the advancing rays of light, we bring back that (Spirit) of your..." (10.58.6).

(d) "Although your spirit have gone far away to the Sun, to the dawn, we bring back that (Spirit) of your..." (10.58.8).

Thus, it is clear that Rishis of Rig Veda reveal that *Atma* or Soul is different from the body, that it does not die and that it moves to *Yama Loka, heaven, advancing Rays of Light, Sun, Earth,* etc.

The science, hesitatingly, has started accepting it now.

This conclusion is further strengthened by Rishi Daman Yaamooyan. He prays to Agni: "Agni, consume him not entirely; afflict him not; scatter not (here and there) his skin or his body...then send him to the Pitras" (10.16.1).

Indirectly Rishi is telling that the five basic elements—Sky, Earth, Agni, Air and Water are burnt by Agni and they return back to their basic elements but the *Atma*, the soul, goes to *Pitra Loka* or *Yama Loka*, to meet the *Pitras* and stays with them.

Rishi Dayananda Saraswati, in his commentary of the above Mantra, though agrees with the basic truth that Atma goes to meet *Pitras* but he slightly differs also.

Sukta 10.16 conveys the above fact in a different way. Mantras 10.14.7, 8 and 10.15.3, 4, 5 also confirm it.

(iii) **Where the dead Pitras go?**

Rishi Yama Vaivashwat reveals: "Worship with oblations *Yama King* (of the Pitras)...who conducts those who are virtuous over the earth, and opens to many the path of heaven" (10.14.1).

When *Yama* is the king of the *Pitras*, then surely all the *Pitras* go to *Yama Loka*.

The same views are expressed in Mantras 10.14.8 and 10.14.10. And by inference, same thing is said in Mantras 10.58.1, 2, 6, 8.

From the reading of these Mantras, it appears *Yama Loka* includes heaven (10.58.2), Rays of light (10.58.6), Sun (10.58.8), etc.

(iv) **Do all Pitras reside at one place?**

Rig Veda reveals that all the Pitras do not reside at one place. Rishis categorise them, as per their deeds on earth, in three categories. For example, Rishi Shankh Yaamaayan classifies them: "Let the lower, the upper, the intermediate Pitra..." (10.15.1).

Thus, it is clear that Pitras have been classified in three categories and accordingly, it seems, they reside at different levels of *Yama Loka*.

Rishi Divya Aangirasa adds: "The donors of the *dakshina* have mounted high in heaven; those who are givers of horses dwell with the Sun; the givers of gold obtain immortality..." (10.107.2).

Thus, it is evident that all Pitras do not reside at one place. They reside at different levels of Yama Loka, as per their deeds on earth.

II. CAN PITRAS VISIT EARTH?

Rig Veda reveals that Pitras can be invited and they do come when called. For example, Rishi Yama Vaivaswat says, "The Angirasas, the Atharvas, the Bhrgus, who are entitled to the Soma, are our recent progenitors; may we ever have a place in the favour of these venerable (Pitras); may we be ever held in their auspicious regard." This clearly shows that Rishi invites the Pitras to take Soma and they do come.

It may be added here that when Pitra, in the form of soul, can go to *Pitra Loka* then certainly it cannot only come back but can also roam about.

Similar views are expressed in Mantras 10.14.5 and 10.15.3, 4, 5 and 8.

III. HAVE PITRAS POWERS?

Rig Veda reveals that Pitras are powerful. They can bless and give wealth, children, health, etc. and can also injure or punish. For example:

Rishi Vasishtha prays: "May the lords of truth for (propitious to) our happiness; may horses, may cattle, (contribute to) our happiness; may the virtuous, the dexterous Rbhus, be to us (for) felicity; may the progenitors be (promoters of) our happiness at the seasons of worship" (7.35.12).

Rishi Shankh Yaamaayan reveals: "Seated in the proximity of the radiant (flames of the altar), bestow riches on the mortal donor (of the oblation); give wealth, Pitras, to his sons; do you who are present grant us vigour" (10.15.7).

Same views have been expressed in Mantras 10.14.6, 10.15.11 and 7.33.4.

To sum up, we can say that we find material on Pitras in Rig Veda. Our dead ancestors are our Pitras. They exist in the form of soul or Atma. They, after death, go to Yama Loka and reside their in upper, middle and lower levels of Yama-Loka as per their deeds on earth. They visit earth on being invited. They have the powers to punish and reward.

APPENDIX I

On Pitras

Sukta

10.14, 10.15 and 10.16

Mantras

1.36.18, 1.10.6.5, 1.109.7, 1.125.5, 6 and 7

6.52.4, 6.75.10

7.33.4, 7.35.12, 7.76.4, 7.104.3, 22

9.113.7, 8, 9 & 11

10.2.7, 10.16.4, 10.18.1, 10.27.1, 10.56.4, 10.87.4, 10.107.2, 10.125.5, 10.135.1, 10.154.5

APPENDIX II

Importance of Shradha

The Hindu families of India, by tradition, for fifteen days in a year, remember their dead forefathers (Pitras) and as a symbol of respect and feeling for them, invite a lady or a male Brahmin, as per the sex of the Pitra, on the *Tithi* (date) of the death day of the Pitra and feed him or her. The Brahmin, before starting eating, offers food in very small quantities to a cow, a crow, a dog and to the Pitra. He invokes Mantras and invites the Pitra. It is said that Pitras do come, enjoy the food and bless the children and help them in times of distress. This, so called ritual, is said to be *Shradha* (i.e. respect) of the Pitra. These fifteen days are called *Pitra-Paksh.*

Today the non-believers in God, the leftists, the socialists, the Congressmen, the anti-Hindu and the persons who proudly call themselves rich, highly educated and elite of the society, scorn at this tradition and call it a wise trick of Brahmins. The author is of the opinion that neither they have tried to study the standard works on the subject nor tried to verify facts with the help of science and psychology. So, it will be better to ignore these critics and try to find out truth.

DOES SOUL EXIST?

Hindu scriptures say that every person has a soul and this soul never dies. It only changes clothes (bodies) after an interval of time. They further say that all the material things, including human body, are made of the permutation and combination of five basic elements—Aakaasha (Sky), Prithvi (Earth), Agni (Fire), Vayu (Air) and Jala (Water).

The Hindu scriptures further reveal that within the outer human body there is a functional body such as lungs, heart, kidneys, nose, ears, eyes, tongue, skin etc. They rightly say that they function with the help of some energy force. These functional parts of the body are also made of the permutation and combination of the five basic elements.

These scriptures also say that every human being has to eat and drink to survive. These eatables, they say, are also made of five basic elements.

After these statements, the scriptures say that there is a soul which is not made of the permutation and combination of five basic elements; it never dies; it is immortal; it only changes bodies and is the source of life and responsible for the functions of the human body.

The modern science earlier, out of ignorance, was not accepting the above facts. But slowly now they are hesitatingly accepting what Hindu scriptures have said, thousands of years back. For example,

(i) The science accepts that the human body is made of five basic elements though they now say that these principal basic elements and their sub-parts are more than 128. But number does not matter.

(ii) The science accepts that inside the human body there are functional parts of the body and they are also made of five basic elements.

(iii) The science also accepts that these functional parts function because of some energy force. They try to measure even the energy waves of the different parts through instruments. For example, they use Electro-Cardiography for measuring heart energy waves, Electro-Ratinography for measuring eyes energy waves and Electro-Encephalography for measuring mind energy waves.

(iv) The science tells us that the food we eat gives us blood, fat, protein, carbohydrates, minerals, vitamins etc. These things form various cells which provide energy to the various parts.

At this, a Hindu enquires that when the supply of five basic elements is available, when eatables are available, when science is able to provide blood, vitamins, minerals etc. to the body and when science has been able to produce spare parts of the human body, who take over the function of the various parts of the body, at the time of crisis, *then why a man dies*? He asks: when science has invented the methods to provide oxygen to body with the help of instruments attached to an oxygen cylinder, when they provide the functioning of lungs with the help of a ventilator, when they provide functioning of kidneys through a Dialysis machine, when they fix eye lenses inside the eyes to improve eyesight etc. etc. then *why the man dies*? Science seems to have no answer.

As this juncture, science was forced to search an answer. In their search, probably out of helplessness, they thought it prudent to test the truth given in scriptures, i.e., SOUL.

Scientists from Russia, England and U.S.A. tried to mesmerise a person and started taking him backward. Questions were asked about the past years of the present life. They were compared with the actual incidents and were found correct. Then they started taking a mesmerised person to the previous lives. In one case they were told that during the world war a few persons ran for safety. They hid themselves in an underground cell. The location of this cell was also told. Later on, it was found to be correct. Not only the underground cell could be found but the skeletons were also discovered. There was no doubt that Hindu scriptures were telling a fact. There is a SOUL which is immortal and takes birth after an interval of time.

Dr. Brien L. Weies, who is a renowned psychiatrist of America, has used the technique of mesmerising his patients and finding out the cause of their tensions and sickness. It helped him. Dr. Weies, on the basis of his experiences, has written a book, *Many Lives, Many Masters.* His studies do not leave any doubt that there is a Soul, that this soul is immortal, that it takes rebirth and that it does not forget the past.

Today science accepts the Hindu view about Soul. It is no more a fiction. Ignorant people of India are at liberty to deny its existence even today.

CAN SOUL COME?

Rishis of Rig Veda have revealed that when a person dies, his soul, which is invisible and weightless, goes to Pitra Loka and normally stays there, in the area which is marked for it, as per its deeds on earth. This soul has the powers to move about. It can come to any place of its choice. It can reach its children when invited by them.

In India, *Tantriks* acquire power to call the souls at will and even talk with them.

Science has yet to verify that souls can move at will. But when they accept that after death soul exists and it does not die and enters into another body then, by inference, they are accepting that the soul moves.

CAN SOUL ACCEPT OFFERINGS?

Rishis have revealed that the soul has the powers to move, see, hear and smell. It can even communicate. How soul does it, is yet to be found out by the science. But ignorance cannot be a cause of its denial.

Today science accepts telepathy. Science also accepts that mind has three parts—conscious, sub-conscious and unconscious. They now accept that till today they have developed methods to awaken the conscious part of mind which is confined only with the material plane. What we call education, training etc. are nothing but the means to develop this conscious part of mind only.

Rishis had developed the techniques to awaken the sub-conscious part of mind. The vision of those persons, who could awaken their sub-conscious mind, gets widened. They can see, hear etc. not only the present, but also the past and even future. The science seems to acknowledge it hesitatingly. For example, they have accepted that when the conscious mind sleeps, sometimes unconscious mind gets awakened. Dream theories of psychologists depend upon this concept. Even science has found out that most of the difficult researches could be done by the Nobel Laureates and others when they got clues in their dreams, i.e., through awakening of sub-conscious mind.

Rishis say that the third part of the mind, the unconscious, is the most important part. Here the soul resides. From here, it provides life to the body, and from here it provides energy to the various functional parts.

Science has yet to explore this area. So, it can be said that when soul can provide life to the body and energy to the various functional parts then certainly it can see, hear, feel and dictate. It is all powerful.

So, when a Pitra is invited and he or she comes, then it can see, hear and smell the offerings made to him or her. Naturally, it gets pleased and blesses its own kith and kin.

SOCIAL IMPORTANCE OF SHRADHA

Rishis, who were scientists, psychologists and social scientists, all rolled in one, tried to achieve another end through this Shradha ritual. They taught youngsters to remember their elders, pay them respect and follow their foot-paths. This strengthened the smallest unit of the society—the family. This made the society virtue oriented. Members learn to be respectful to elders. They love them, remember their good deeds, donate in their memory and pray. It is thanksgiving.

Chapter 19

Spiritual Gods in Rig Veda

A reading of Rig Veda, with the help of research methodology and science, makes it clear that the wise Rishis of Rig Veda first found out the five basic natural phenomena, which later they called gods, viz., Aakaasha (Sky), Prithvi (Earth), Agni (Energy, of all types), Varuna (Water) and Vayu (Air of all varieties). Their studies revealed that the permutations and combinations of these five basic elements help in creating all the material things. These Rishis raised these five basic elements and their associates to the status of gods for very good reasons. They made intensive studies to know about them—their source, their traits, their laws etc. These Rishis, afterwards, found out that all the material things—dead or living, after a period of time, start decaying and ultimately die. After death they again disintegrate in the five basic elements. So, naturally a curiosity should have arisen among these Rishis to know why all the material things, specially living bodies, who are made of five elements, die even when these five basic elements are available in good quantities? What is there which keeps the living bodies functional? Researches revealed them that there is a new element, which when leaves the body, death occurs. They called it Soul or *Atma*.

When due to further researches, the truth dawned on the Rishis that there is something like a Soul or *Atma*, who continues to leave a body to re-enter in another body, after an interval of time, then the natural curiosity arose to know: where the ATMA goes after leaving a body? The studies revealed that this tiny, invisible ATMA goes to a place which Rishis called PITRA-LOKA. This led to the indepth studies of YAMA and YAMA-LOKA or PITRA-LOKA.

These studies of Atma opened up the doors of new knowledge. These Rishis could find out that the soul is immortal and that there are other gods related with Atma, whom they named as Yama, Brahamma, Rudra (Shiva) and Vishnu. Once they could identify gods connected with soul, the question arose to find out their interrelations. They could discover that they are interrelated with each other. The source of *Atma*, they found out, is *Parmatma*. (More about it later.)

While Rishis, trying to find out more facts about *Atma*, *Parmatma*, Yama, Rudra (Shiva), Brahamma and Vishnu, another element struck them. They discovered a new important element which they named as *Manas* (desires). Rishis Bandhu, Subandhu, Shrut Bandhu and Gopayan or Lopayan have offered one full Sukta (10.54) to *Manas*. They reveal that this element, *Manas*, is very erratic. It runs from one place to another very quickly. Sometimes it goes to heaven and the other second it visits oceans, Sun, mountains, different parts of earth and space. These Rishis found out that without perfect control of this *Manas*, one cannot feel *Atma* or *Parmatma*. Only when *Manas* is perfectly channelised towards *Atma* or *Parmatma*, one can realise them. It is a media to reach Spirit, hidden in the body and also at a central place, called Vishnu.

It is unfortunate that foreign scholars like H.H. Wilson, R.T.H. Griffith etc. could not differentiate between *Manas* and Spirit and consider them synonyms. It is only Rishi Dayananda who has mentioned their difference.

After this brief narration of history of finding out spirit and its associated gods, it will be proper to discuss them here, one by one.

(1) KING YAMA

In Rig Veda, *Yama*, though deals with *Atma*, is called a king. The scholars should answer.

In Rig Veda we find the following Suktas and Mantras offered to King Yama.

ON KING YAMA

S.No.	*Sukta*	*Mantra*
1.	10.10	1.35.6
2.	10.14	1.38.5
3.	10.135	1.163.2
4.	10.154	7.76.4

5. — 9.113.8
6. — 10.13.4
7. — 10.16.9
8. — 10.17.1
9. — 10.18.13
10. — 10.24.5
11. — 10.52.3
12. — 10.64.3
13. — 10.92.11
14. — 10.97.16
15. — 10.165.4

Out of all the Rishis of Rig Veda, only 18, i.e., 4.4% have offered their Suktas and Mantras to King Yama. This, as per the writer, shows that the Rishis, first, were engrossed in finding out the truths about natural phenomena gods and only after they had finished their studies about them, that their attention was drawn towards the Spirit and Spiritual gods—*Parmatma* (Vishnu), *Atma, Rudra, Brahamma* and *Yama*. So, the number of Rishis, who studied this new sphere, is not only small but their names also show that they were not very famous and were of a later period. One thing more. The families of Rishi Vaivashwat and Yaamaayan, it appears, have made special studies of this difficult region.

The name of King Yama's father is Vivasvat (10.14.5) and of mother Saranyu, the daughter of Tvashta (10.17.1, 2). On the basis of the name of the father of Yama, he is called Yama and his sister, Yami. It is strange that Yami, the sister, wanted to marry her brother, Yama but Yama was not agreeable to it (10.10). Scholars should try to solve this riddle.

King Yama resides in *Yama-Loka.* Rishis reveal that *Antariksha* (i.e., the region upto 300 miles above the earth) is the gateway for *Yama-Loka* (1.35.56, 9.113.8). By inference, it implies that *Pitra-Loka* should be the lower part of *Aakaasha* (Sky), but above *Antariksha* (which is also a part of the sky) where King Yama and the souls, who leave the bodies, reside. In Yama Loka, pipe is always sounding (10.135.7).

King Yama has associations with various gods (10.135.1). He enjoys with god Varuna (god of water) (10.14.7), Vrahaspati (10.13.4, 10.14.3), god Surya (Sun) (1.163.2) and god Agni (Fire), who are his friends. The scholars should try to know their common links.

Whosoever dies, his soul goes to *Yama-Loka* (10.13.4) Yama sends his messengers—pigeon, owl (10.165.4) and four eyed two dogs (10.14.11) to fetch them. (Here one will like to know whether it means to take out the soul from the body or to take it from outside the body to Yama-Loka, or both. Yama uses fetters to bring soul. These souls also go by the same route by which their forefathers had travelled. King Yama knows the deeds of the dead and so gives places to these souls as per their good or bad deeds (10.14.2, 9, 10.15.4). He provides residences to them (10.18.3).

It is thus apparent that Rishis of Rig Veda associate life and death with the soul and also reveal that these souls have powers to travel—they go to Yama-Loka to come back. They also assign the function of taking these souls to *Yama-Loka*. Obviously, King Yama does not take out souls from the living beings—flora, fauna and human beings.

(2) RUDRA-DEVA

A.A. Macdonell opines that god Rudra is associated with Antariksha (the lower portion of the sky which is upto 300 miles above earth) where there is air and gravitation force of earth. This Antariksha and its upper part is Aakaasha (Sky). The author feels that god Rudra should be a god associated with the portion of the sky which is above the earth's gravitation zone.

It is said that in Sanskrit, every word has a meaning but the meaning of 'Rudra' is not clear. Some scholars opine that Rudra means made of metal, some say it means 'crying' and some others say that it means "Super-natural Power", "Soul" or "Air".

The Suktas and Mantras, which have been offered to god Rudra, have been given below:

ON RUDRA

S. No.	*Sukta*	*Mantra*
1.	1.114	1.43.1, 2, 4-6
2.	2.33	5.5.3
3.	7.46	5.42.11
4.	—	7.59.12

Out of all the Rishis of Rig Veda, only 6 Rishis, i.e., 1.56% have offered their Suktas and Mantras to god Rudra. This shows that very few Rishis could discover facts about god Rudra. This confirms the earlier view that the gods related with Atma (soul) were discovered at a later stage. So, they are Spiritual Gods.

The author failed to identify god Rudra as a Natural Phenomena God because even now science is not much aware of this spiritual area though they are trying to know more and more about it.

Rishis of Rig Veda pray Rudra that he may not kill them, their children and animals but may protect them (1.114.4, 7, 8; 2.33.14, 7.46.2, 3, 4). He may not catch them with his fetters (7.59.12). This shows that god Rudra must also be associated with taking out life because death, as per Hindu philosophy, means the soul going out from the body.

A question arises: Are King Yama and god Rudra synonym? If not, what is the difference between the two?

The considered view of the author is that both are different having different functions. God Rudra takes out the soul from the body and there his work ends. Thereafter, King Yama takes over. He takes this soul to his own Yama-Loka and allots it a living place, as per the deeds.

In this sense also god Rudra is a Spiritual God.

The colour of god Rudra is yellow (2.33.4,

5.15.18). He is as radiant as god Surya (Sun), i.e., he glitters (1.43.5, 1.114.5) or he is of a white complexion (2.33.8). God Rudra has braided hair (1.114.5). He has a soft belly, a tawny blue and handsome chain (2.33.5). God Rudra has "joy dispensing hands", which are the healer and delighter (2.33.7). He is mighty (1.43.3; 2.33.3) who always remains youthful (2.33.11).

Rudras keep a thunderbolt (2.33.3). He keeps weapon to destroy heroes, and slay men (1.114.10). He has the strong bow and arrows (5.42.11). They are blazing and are discharged from heaven (7.46.3). They kill everybody, friends and enemies (1.114.1, 2, 3). This description testifies the author's inference that it is god Rudra, who kills a living being, i.e., takes out soul from the body and it is king Yama who takes them to Yama-Loka.

Rudra is said to be the father of the Maruts (1.114.6, 2.33.1, 3.42.2). The concept is not very clear. That part of Vayu (Air), which moves or circulates, has been called god Marudagan. Their number is said to be 49. The scholars should explain the relationship between the two.

God Rudra, Rishis inform, is a noted physician (1.43.4, 1.114.5, 2.33.2, 4, 7; 5.42.11, 5.46.2). He is physician of physicians (2.33.4). Rishis pray and request him to give them, to their children and even to their tame animals and birds a healthy life, a long life (1.43.4, 1.114.2, 4, 5, 2.33.1, 2, 4, 7, 7.46.2). God Rudra grants them their prayers. The author failed to find out the relationship between god Rudra and his curing talents. The scholars should try to find it out.

In the end, it can be concluded that god Rudra is a spiritual God who was discovered by the Rishis at a later stage.

The description of god Rudra and king Yama makes it clear, why one is a god and the other is a king—king of Yama-Loka.

(3) GOD BRAHAMMA (PRAJAPATI)

Today god Brahamma is known as one of the trinity. He is associated with soul. He is described as one who feeds living beings. Some scholars describe him as Prajapati also. (Rig Veda describes Prajapati as a King or a Priest of Gods.)

Search for Suktas and Mantras on Prajapati (god Brahamma) in Rig Veda revealed the following Mantras and Suktas only: 1.28.9, 1.71.5, 4.53.2, 8.87.2, 10.18.14, 10.61.5, 6, 7, 10.81.3, 10.82, 10.169.4, 10.170.4, 10.184.1.

Reading of these Suktas and Mantras revealed that hardly any substantial matter is found in Rig Veda about god Brahamma. The above references are of Prajapati who is a king or a priest and not a god. He has nothing to do with feeding the living beings.

Sanskrit scholars opine that Sukta 10.121 which has been offered to "Ka" (Prajapati), clearly is related with god Brahamma. Let us see:

10.121.1	He was the sole lord of created beings.
10.121.2	He is the giver of soul.
10.121.3	He is the sole king of the giver of breath.

10.121.4 He, with his two arms, protects the world.

10.121.5 He is the maker of Aakaasha (Sky), Prithvi (Earth), Heaven and Solar System.

10.121.6-10 Hymns are offered in his praise.

The above Sukta 10.121 only praises the Super Power, Parmatma and, it is apparent, is not concerned with god Brahamma.

Natural phenomena gods—Sky, Earth, Agni, Vayu and Varuna provide the basic elements by which different forms can be created. It is the wise craftsmen like Vishvakarma, Tvastha, Ribhugan who assemble these basic elements in different permutations and combinations and create flora, fauna and all human beings. To make these creations living, another set of gods are required—one who generates Soul Energy, one who puts a tiny part of it in the bodies and the other who takes it out.

It can, thus, be concluded, that we do not find any description of god Brahamma as a feeder of living beings in Rig Veda. But a conjecture can be made that god Brahamma is one who introduces the tiny, weightless and formless spirit or soul into the living beings.

(4) BHAGWAN VISHNU

In Rig Veda very few Suktas and Mantras have been offered to Bhagwan Vishnu. But a reading of them makes it abundantly clear that he is a superior god, god of all gods and a Super Power, a Parmatma.

The Suktas and Mantras, which have been offered to Bhagwan Vishnu, are:

ON BHAGWAN VISHNU

S. No.	*Suktas*	*Mantras*
1.	1.154	1.22.16, 17-21
2.	1.156	1.155, 1-3, 4-6
3.	7.100	7.99, 1-3, 7, 4-6

Today and in Puranic Period also, Bhagwan Vishnu has been given the maximum importance. He is said to be the creator and feeder of all the living beings. In spite of this unique importance, why only three Rishis have offered their three Suktas and 17 Mantras to Bhagwan Vishnu? The author feels that it was only in the later period of Rig Veda that Spiritual Gods could be traced out and also amongst them, probably Vishnu could be traced out in the last.

A reading of the above mentioned Suktas and Mantras provides the following information on Bhagwan Vishnu:

1. No information is found in Rig Veda about the physical features of Bhagwan Vishnu. Why this difference with the Natural Phenomena Gods? Is it because Atma has no form and so all the spiritual gods have no physical features.
2. No description is available about Bhagwan Vishnu's weapons, etc.

3. It is said that Bhagwan Vishnu resides in Aakaasha (Sky) or Heaven (1.22.20, 1.155.6). Rishis have not told clearly whether it is Sky or Heaven.

4. Lot has been talked about the three feet of Bhagwan Vishnu (1.22.16, 17, 18; 1.154.2, 3, 1.155.5, 7.100.3). Different scholars have given different meanings to the three feet. Some are:

   (a) Bhagwan Vishnu, it is said, has created three worlds (Loka)—Aakaasha (Sky), Prithvi (Earth) and Paataala (Below earth). So, his each leg represents one world (1.154.133). Rishis further reveal that an ordinary person can only see his two feet—Aakaasha (Sky) and Prithvi (Earth) (1.155.5, 7.99.1).

   (b) Bhagwan Vishnu's three feet represent three Gunas—Sataguna, Rajoguna and Tamoguna (1.154.4). Bhagwan is Triguni. It is further said that these three Gunas are represented respectively by the light of the Sun or Agni, Water and Prithvi (Earth).

5. Bhagwan Vishnu not only creates but also feeds (1.155.4, 1.156.1, 4, 5).

   He fulfils the desires of disciples. He gives in accordance to the deeds of the disciples (1.155.2; 7.100.1, 2).

6. Bhagwan Vishnu is Divine (1.156.5), i.e., none knows when was he born. He is immortal.

7. Bhagwan Vishnu is very powerful. He rotates a period (kala) in 94 sub-circles (1.155.6), i.e., years, months, fortnights, days, minutes, seconds, seasons, two limits

of the Sun—Tropic of Cancer and Tropic of Capricorn and *Rashis*. It means Bhagwan Vishnu is the controller of time.

The above information about Bhagwan Vishnu is not sufficient to reveal his entire personality but is sufficient to establish him as a Super-power or *Bhagwan*. It is said that Bhagwan Vishnu's, only a microscopic part (or as some say reflection) is *Atma* which provides life to the vegetables, birds, animals, man and other living beings.

This inference about Bhagwan Vishnu gets confirmed by the most important Sukta (10.90) of Rig Veda, viz., Sukta Brahama. It clarifies that there is no difference between Super Power, called Parmatma or known as Bhagwan Vishnu. He is the creator and also life giver. From him everything is born—gods, horses, animals, cows, goats, sheeps, different Varnas—Brahmin, Kshatriya, Vaish and Daas (later called Shudra), Sun, Moon, Agni, Air, Heaven, Prithvi, etc.

Certainly Bhagwan Vishnu is Parmatma.

It may be conjectured that Parmatma Vishnu is the centre of Soul or Atma Energy. In the modern terminology he can be compared with a generator, House of Soul-Energy.

In the end, it can be concluded that in Rig Veda, amongst the Spiritual Gods, we only find Raja Yama, god Rudra, Bhagwan Vishnu and Brahamma.

Chapter 20

God Craftsmen: Vishvakarma, Tvashta and Ribhugan

Before writing about Vishvakarma, Tvashta and Ribhugan, it is desirable to clarify the following things:

1. A.A. Macdonell in Vedic Mythology categorises Vishvakarma and Tvashta as *Amurta* gods and Ribhugan as *Avar* god. On the basis of the studies of Rig Veda, with the help of other authorities, the author has reached the well thought out conclusion that these three are not gods but only excellent craftsmen.

2. A reading of Rig Veda clearly demonstrates that a few Rishis found out the basic natural phenomena—Aakaasha (Sky), Prithvi (Earth), Agni (Fire), Varuna (Water) and Vayu (Air). They called all of them gods. They could also find out their associate gods.

(All this has been discussed earlier.) These wise Rishis could also discuss that all the material things, including the bodies of the living beings, are made of the permutation and combination of the basic natural phenomena gods. In course of time, they found out that in spite of the availability of all the basic natural phenomena in sufficient quantities, the living beings die. This led them to find out the cause. The searches helped them to know that there is another factor, which they called Atma (soul), which is responsible to keep living bodies alive. This clue led them to discover the source of the soul. So, they gave us another set-up of gods which the author has named as Spiritual Gods. (Discussed earlier.)

This reading of the gods forced the author to search out the missing link.

There are five basic elements available to make the forms of bodies and there is also a soul which is available to make the bodies alive. But where are the bodies, the structures? A reading of Rig Veda showed that the wise Rishis have also given the descriptions of the excellent craftsmen who make the different types of structures or forms. They have also been raised to godhood. The first craftsman was Vishvakarma, thereafter Tvashta and lastly Ribhugan, whose number is three.

3. A reading of Suktas and Mantras on Vishvakarma shows that they were the first inventor craftsmen who gave shape or body structures to all the material things—living or lifeless, soon after *Pralaya* (Doomsday), i.e., they were the first creator but they disappear after the world is made functional, after each *Pralaya* (Doomsday).

4. Similar to Vishvakarma, the next craftsman, Tvashta, who took over from Vishvakarma, is an equally good craftsman. This is not clear why Vishvakarma left and how and why Tvashta was born.

5. It appears, as the work-load increased, Tvashta alone was not able to cope with the work-load. So, naturally, he trained up people into good craftsmen. These disciples were three, called Ribhugan.

After this brief narration, a list of all the Suktas and Mantras is being given on Vishvakarma, Tvashta and Ribhugan.

1. VISHVAKARMA

S. No.	*Sukta*	*Mantra*
1.	10.81	—
2.	10.82	—

2. TVASHTA

S. No.	*Sukta*	*Mantra*
1.	—	1.13.10
2.	—	1.15.3
3.	—	1.22.9
4.	—	1.80.14
5.	—	1.85.9
6.	—	1.88.9
7.	—	2.3.9
8.	—	2.36.3
9.	—	3.4.9
10.	—	3.54.12
11.	—	3.55.19

12.	—	5.5.9
13.	—	5.31.3
14.	—	6.47.19
15.	—	6.49.9
16.	—	7.34.21
17.	—	8.29.3
18.	—	9.5.9
19.	—	10.2.7
20.	—	10.10.5
21.	—	10.10.17
22.	—	10.18.6
23.	—	10.49.10
24.	—	10.53.9
25.	—	10.70.9
26.	—	10.92.11
27.	—	10.110.9
28.	—	10.184.1

3. RIBHUGAN

S. No.	*Sukta*	*Mantra*
1.	—	1.16.1
2.	—	3.60.1-4
3.	—	7.48.1-3
4.	4.33	10.176.1
5.	4.34	—
6.	4.35	—
7.	4.36	—
8.	4.37	—

On the basis of the above three tables, some questions crop up:

1. Why only two Suktas and no Mantra have been offered on Vishvakarma?

   Why only one Rishi, whose name is also Vishvakarma Bhaum, out of all the Rishis of Rig Veda, has offered only two Suktas on Vishvakarma? Does it not show that Rishis of Rig Veda could not find out much material on this first inventor craftsman?

2. Is it not strange that not a single Sukta has been offered on Tvashta. What does it show? Out of all the Rishis of Rig Veda only 23 Rishis have offered only 28 Mantras, i.e., most of the Rishis, except a few, have offered only one Mantra each on Tvashta. Probably these Rishis failed to find out more facts about Tvashta. One thing more struck the author. Two members of the families of each of the Rishi Atrey, Rishi Bharadwaj, Rishi Yamayan and Rishi Vishvamitra gave Mantras on Tvashta. Does it show these families were trying to specialise on him?

3. Only five Rishis have offered 5 Suktas and 9 Mantras to three Ribhugan. Why is it so? Out of these five Rishis also, maximum contribution is of three Rishis—Rishis Gratsamada, Rishi Medhatithi Kandav and Rishi Vasishtha. Why is it so?

It is expected that the scholars, specially of Sanskrit, will give us answers to these questions.

Now efforts are being made to present the facts about these three wise craftsmen—Vishvakarma, Tvashta and Ribhugan, one after another, as found in Rig Veda.

(1) VISHVAKARMA

In twenty-first century India, Vishvakarma is worshipped as a first engineer who gave birth to Industrialisation in India (through crafts). Here efforts have been made to know what Rig Veda had to say about him.

Rishis of Rig Veda opine that Vishvakarma was the first craftsman of the world, who created all the material things, living or otherwise, after each Pralaya (10.81.1, 7, 10.82.1, 2, 3). Requests have been made to him to create material goods of all qualities—good, medium and poor (10.81.5). These Rishis go to the extent of saying that he created Prithvi (Earth), Aakaasha (Sky) and even the Directions (East, West, North, South, etc.) (10.82.1). Probably, this exaggeration was a style of Rishis to emphasize an idea.

Rishis of Rig Veda have described the physical features of almost all gods but they do not mention anything about the face, colour, nose, hands, etc. of Vishvakarma. Why? Is it because they do not consider him a god?

Rishis reveal that Vishvakarma is gifted with "a comprehensive mind and manifold greatness" who could create all the material things, living or otherwise (10.82.2).

Rishis want to know which wood and of which forest is used by Vishvakarma (obviously for wood articles) (10.81.4).

Rishis do not give any details of the tools used by Vishvakarma for manufacturing different things by using different raw materials such as wood, metals etc. They do not even mention about his place of working (10.81.2).

Vishvakarma can see everywhere and can reach everywhere very fast (10.81.3). One is not able to understand the meaning of it.

The above description does not reveal much about Vishvakarma except that he is an excellent craftsman and produces every material thing, for some time, after each pralaya.

Here a very pertinent question arises. Rishi Vishvakarma Bhaum reveals that Vishvakarma, the wonderful craftsman, is a creator. On the other hand, dozens of other Rishis of Rig Veda also opine that god Brahamma is also a creator. Then the question is: Are both of them synonyms? Or are there some differences between the two? The considered opinion of the author is that Vishvakarma, the craftsman, is a creator in the sense that he produces the structures or various forms of all the material things or living things with the help of five basic elements—sky, earth, fire, water and air—like arms, chariots, animals, vegetation, man, etc. All these things remain lifeless. It is god Brahamma who provides soul to some structures, who then become living. God Brahamma is a creator in the sense that he provides life. So, he is called a god while the poor Vishvakarma remains a craftsman only.

(2) TVASHTA

The Rishis, who have offered their Mantras to

Tvashta, have nowhere described physical features of Tvashta, as they have done in case of other gods. The only exception is that they give adjectives to the hands such as "the dexterous handed" (3.54.12), "the well handed" (6.49.9). The attitude of these Rishis is similar to that of the Rishi Vishvedeva Bhaum, who has also not described the features of Vishvakarmas.

In Rig Veda, Tvashta has been called 'Divine' (3.54.11, 10.92.11, 10.110.9) but not god. How to reconcile both?

A Rishi reveals that by the roar of god Indra, even Tvashta "shook with fear". This shows that in spite of Tvashta being "divine" he is not fearless.

Rishi Garga Bharadwaja reveals that Tvashta is yoking his car (6.47.19). This shows that he travels with speed.

Tvashta has been described as a master (in fashioning) the forms, an able and skilful artificer, a renowned and a glorious creator and a person who fabricates the members in the womb (1.188.9, 3.54.12, 6.49.9, 10.27, 10.18.6, 10.53.9, 10.189.1).

No information has been given about the tools of Tvashta by which he fabricates different material forms except that he possesses an axe (8.29.3, 10.53.9).

Tvashta is the first craftsman who can produce material things of different forms (of course after Vishvakarma) (6.49.9). Here are a few illustrations of his creations:

1. Tvashta manufactured one radiant thunderbolt for god Indra (5.31.4) and also another many-bladed thunderbolt (1.85.9).

2. Tvashta produces the (forms of various) food (6.49.9). Food includes several eatables such as wheat, gram, barley, etc. It means, he, treating the seeds of wheat, gram, barley, etc. as womb, creates the various forms of plants. After some time, as per Rishis of Rig Veda, god Brahamma gives them life.

3. Tvashta not only creates various eatables but he also creates various forms of birds and animals. He makes all of them distinct (1.188.9).

4. Yami reveals that "the divine omniform generator Tvashta, the progenitor, made us two husband and wife, even in the womb" (10.10.5). So, like food, birds and animals etc. Tvashta gives various forms of children of man in the womb. Brahamma, it can be said, gives life to these structures of children after three months. Various Rishis say the same thing in their own style (3.4.9, 3.55.19, 5.5.9). Modern science accepts that various forms, sex, etc. are made in the womb.

Summing up, it can be said that while Vishvakarma creates various forms or structures of material and living things, only after Pralaya (Doomsday), for a short duration, Tvashta takes over the work thereafter. And god Brahamma gives life to them after a period of time.

(3) RIBHUGAN

Ribhugan, as per Rishis of Rig Veda, are the

sons of Sudhanvan (1.161.2, 3.60.1; 4.33.5; 4.35.1, 8; 1.110.2). Ribhugan are three. Their names are: Ribhu, Vibhva and Vaaja. The eldest of them was Ribhu and so all the three are known after his name. All the three were born as men but because of their excellent deeds, they were raised to Divinity (1.110.4; 4.33.2; 4.35.8; 4.60.3). To prove it, the Rishis show them in the company of various gods like Indra, Ashvins, Mitra, Varuna, Aditi etc. (1.110.9, 1.11.1, 4.33.2). No justification has been given to this friendly relation of Ribhugan with different gods. It may be just a way to glorify the Ribhugan.

In Rig Veda, like Vishvakarma and Tvashta, no description is found of the physical features of the Ribhugan. Only at one place Rishi Vaamdeva Gautam says that they have "jaws of iron" (4.37.4). Probably, this is a style to narrate their physical strength.

All the three Ribhugan are disciples and co-workers to Tvashta (1.20.6). All the three are hardworking and efficient craftsmen (4.35.2, 3, 9).

No description is found in Rig Veda of the tools of Ribhugan. There is a strange similarity about Vishvakarma, Tvashta and Ribhugan. There must be some reason for it. Scholars should try to find it out.

These three Ribhugan, who are excellent craftsmen, have given form and structures to all the material things with the help of five basic elements—Sky, Earth, Fire, Water and Air. Some illustrations of their wonderful creations are:

1. All the three Ribhu reached a Yagya-Shala. They found that there is only one ladle. Probably, it was for Tvashta. So, they cut it and made four out of it—one for each one of them (1.20.6, 1.110.3, 5, 1.161.2, 9, 3.60.2, 4.35.2, 3, 4; 4.36.4).

2. Ribhus created chariots (1.20.3, 1.111.1, 1.161.3, 4.33.8). They manufactured a unique chariot for Ashvins of triangular shape, with three wheels and three compartments to sit (4.36.1, 2).

3. They manufactured various arms (1.111.3, 4.34.9).

4. Ribhu created the form and structure of a horse for god Indra (1.20.2, 1.111.1, 1.161.3, 3.60.2, 4.33.10). They created two forms of horses out of one (1.161.7).

5. Ribhus prepared the forms and structures of cows (1.20.3, 1.110.8, 1.161.3, 7, 4.33.8).

6. They germinated grass from earth (1.161.11). They made the earth fertile and gave forms to various foods (1.111.2, 3, 4.33.7, 4.36.8). It is probably for this reason that Rishis beg corn or food from them. (They probably forgot that the various forms produced by them are lifeless. They have only form.)

7. Ribhus, Rishis say, made old young (1.20.4, 1.111.1, 4.34.9, 4.35.5, 4.36.3). Ribhus have been described by the wise Rishis as able craftsmen who could only give form and not life. So, this seems to be an exaggeration to show their dexterity.

8. Ribhus, like Tvashta, with the help of the five basic elements—Sky, Earth, Fire, Water and Air, manufacture the various forms and structures of men. Later, god Brahamma gives them spirit or soul

and makes them living. So, Rishis request Ribhus to fabricate for them progeny (4.36.9).

In the end, it can be said that wise Rishis first found out the five basic elements and raised all of them to the status of gods. Thereafter, they discovered that there is a soul which makes various forms alive. They found out various spiritual gods like Yama, Rudra, Brahamma and Vishnu. Now only the connecting link was missing. Who makes various forms out of five basic elements? Search led them to discover three excellent craftsmen—Vishvakarma, Tvashta and Ribhugan, who create various forms and structures. Thus, they succeeded in unearthing a very great and important truth.

BOOK III

Other Gods

Chapter 21

Vishvedeva

While reading Rig Veda, I found that a large number of Rishis have offered any number of Suktas and Mantras to Vishvedeva. Naturally, therefore, I thought it desirable to find out who Vishvedeva is? What are his characteristics? What are his doings? And what is his place in the galaxy of Devatas?

I collected all the Suktas and Mantras that have been offered to Vishvedeva. They have been given in Appendix I.

Appendix I shows that 53 Rishis of Rig Veda, i.e., 13.7%, have offered their full Suktas or Mantras to Vishvedeva. This is a good number in comparison with Suktas and Mantras offered to other deities.

I started the study with the presumption that Vishvedeva will also be a god like other deities—Aditi, Diti, Surya, Mitra, Usha, Savita, Bhaga, Ashvins, Aakaasha, Prithvi, Vayu, Varuna, etc. to name a few and so it will not be difficult to know his virtues and field of activity. But this presumption proved to be wrong. It appears *Vishvedeva is no single god but he represents all gods.* This conclusion has been made on several counts. First, most of the Rishis do not even mention once the name of Vishvedeva in the Suktas which they have offered to him. Instead, several deities have been invited. Second, several Rishis use the word *Devagana* or *Devataas,* which certainly is plural, denoting more than one deity or a collection of gods. Third, Rishi Vasishtha mentions all the thirtythree deities (8.28.1) but not Vishvedeva. Fourth, the Sanskrit word Vishve has two meanings—one pertaining to world and second more than one.[1] Here, it is used in the second sense. Thus, it can be concluded that Vishvedeva represents all the deities of Rig Veda.

A question can be asked: Why wise Rishis of Rig Veda decided to offer their Suktas and Mantras collectively to all the Devatas of Rig Veda? What is the rationale behind it?

It is clear that wise Rishis wanted to convey several important ideas by creating Vishvedeva as a representative of all the Devatas.[2] Some of them seem to be:

1. *All the Devatas of Rig Veda are complementary to each other,* they are not competitive. These wise Rishis have called the five basic elements—Aakaasha, Prithvi,

---

[1]Editor, Jai Shankar Joshi, Halayudh-Kosha, Saraswati Bhawan, Varanasi, 1879.

[2]Rishis have some different ideas about Vishnu, Rudra, Brahamma, etc. Probably they are not represented by Vishvedeva.

Agni, Vayu and Varuna—as Devatas. These Devatas are natural phenomena. The Rishis have further conveyed, in their own way, that the permutation and combination of these five basic elements (*Pancha-Tatva*) creates all the material things and also provides subsistence to them. Naturally, it means that these Devatas are complementary to each other and not inimical to one another. None of them has any conflict of interest with others. So, Rishis in Suktas, offered to Vishvedeva, have invited each and every Devata to come and accept Soma and bless them. This shows their mutual cordiality. From this it may be inferred:

That everyone is allowed to select a god for himself. This selection, it seems to imply, should be on the basis of the similarity of the characteristics of the selected Devata and the inborn traits, instincts, nature etc. of the worshipper. This is likely to be more beneficial and peace giver. Immediately the wave-lengths of the two will become the same.

That everyone is allowed to pray, besides his principal deity, any other deity or more than one deity. There is no conflict.

That when the Devatas are friends to each other, naturally, their followers cannot be inimical to each other. There is no scope for crusades or fights between the followers of the different sects like Shia and Sunni. History of Hindu Dharma bears it out.

2. All the Devatas are equal. None of them is superior or inferior. The way the Rishis have invited the gods to come and accept Soma, clearly, demonstrates that

there is no order of preference or priority. All have been treated alike.

3. All Devatas are merciful. Rishis invite them and request them to give them wealth, cows, horses, other animals, houses, health, good children and anything and everything which they need. And these Devatas, in their goodness, kindness and benevolence, oblige.

A question may be ventured here, why these Devatas are kind-hearted and benevolent? Do they get pleased only by the offerings of Soma and give what is demanded? Is there any other message which the Rishis tried to convey? Let us try to understand.

Prayers imply that you admit that the Deity is superior and more powerful than you and that you want to humour him and to win his blessings and favours. This indirectly also means that you will obey his rules, his guidelines, his dictates. You will always remain subordinate to him and his will, you will try to win his blessings by working according to his wishes, i.e., with his cooperation and will never try to insult him, i.e., exploit him beyond a reasonable limit or pollute him. When these rules of the game are observed strictly then the Devata smiles on you and gives you what you want. In other words, prayers teach us to be contented, self-disciplined, work in cooperation with the Devata (i.e., a natural phenomenon, which he is), never try to overexploit nature or pollute it. This is a key to happiness.

Thus, it is clear that Vishvedeva is no Devata. He is a representative of all devatas—a unique character created by Rishis to give very useful messages to humanity so that they can remain healthy, happy and contented.

APPENDIX I
VISHVEDEVA

S. No.	*Suktas*	*Rishi*
1.	1.14	Medhaatithi Kaandava
2.	1.89	Gautamo Raahugana
3.	1.90	Gautamo Raahugana
4.	1.105	Kutsa Aangirasa
5.	1.106	Kutsa Aangirasa
6.	1.107	Kutsa Aangirasa
7.	1.122	Kakshivaana Dairdhtamas (Aushija)
8.	1.186	Agastya
9.	2.29	Kurmo Gaartsamada
10.	2.31	Gratsamado Bhaargava Shaunak
11.	3.54	Prajaapatirvaachya, Prajaapati Vaishwaamitra
12.	3.56	Prajaapatirvaachya, Prajaapati Vaishwaamitra
13.	3.57	Prajaapatirvaachya, Prajaapati Vaishwaamitra
14.	4.55	Vaamdeva
15.	5.41	Atri Bhaum
16.	5.43	Atri Bhaum
17.	5.44	Avtasaar Kaashyap, Rishyau Drashtilingaa
18.	5.45	Sadaaprana Aatreya
19.	5.47	Pratiratha Aatreya

20.	5.48	Pratibhaanu Aatreya
21.	5.49	Pratiprabha Aatreya
22.	5.50	Swasti Aatreya
23.	5.51	Swasti Aatreya
24.	6.49	Rigishwaa Bhaaradwaaja
25.	6.50	Rigishwaa Bhaaradwaaja
26.	6.51	Rigishwaa Bhaaradwaaja
27.	6.52	Rigishwaa Bhaaradwaaja
28.	7.35	Vasishtha
29.	7.36	Vasishtha
30.	7.37	Vasishtha
31.	7.39	Vasishtha
32.	7.42	Vasishtha
33.	7.43	Vasishtha
34.	8.27	Manu Vaivaswata
35.	8.28	Manu Vaivaswata
36.	8.29	Manu Vaivaswata and Kashyapa Maareecha
37.	8.30	Manu Vaivaswata
38.	8.83	Kuseedee Kaandava
39.	10.31	Kavasha Ailusha
40.	10.32	Kavasha Ailusha
41.	10.35	Lusha Dhaanaakaa
42.	10.36	Lusha Dhaanaakaa
43.	10.56	Uvahadukha Vaamdeva
44.	10.57	Bandhu, Subandhu, Shrutbandhu, Viprabandhu (Gopayana)
45.	10.61	Naabhaanedishtha Maanava
46.	10.64	Gai Plaata
47.	10.65	Vasukarna Vaasukra

48.	10.66	Vasukarna Vaasukra
49.	10.92	Shaaryaata Maanava
50.	10.93	Taanva Paartha
51.	10.101	Budha Saumya
52.	10.109	Juhoo Brahamjaayaa
53.	10.114	Dharma Taapas
54.	10.126	Anhaumuk Vaamdeva
55.	10.128	Vihvya Aangirasa
56.	10.137	Saptarishigana
57.	10.141	Agni Taapas
58.	10.157	Saadhan Bhauvan
59.	10.164	Prachetaa Aangirasa
60.	10.181	Pratha Vaasishtha

Mantras

1.	1.3.7-9	Madhuchandaa Vaishvaamitra
2.	1.23. 10-12	Medhaatithi Kaandava
3.	1.139.1	Paruchepau Devodaasi
4.	1.164. 1-41	Deerghatamaa Auchathya
5.	3.8.9, 10	Vishwaamitra Gaathir
6.	3.20.1-5	Gaathi Kaushika
7.	5.26.9	Vasooyu Aatreya
8.	5.46.1-6	Pratishatra Aatreya
9.	6.21.9, 11	Bharadwaajo Vaarhaspatya
10.	7.48.4	Vasishtha
11.	7.50.3	Vasishtha
12.	8.25. 10-12	Vishvamanaa Vaivashva

13.	8.54.3, 4	Maatrishvaa Kaandava
14.	8.69.11	Priyamedha Aangirasa
15.	9.67.27	Vasishtha
16.	10.33.1	Kavash Ailusha
17.	10.62.1-6	Naabhaanedishtha Maanava
18.	10.63. 1-14, 17	Gai Plaata

Chapter 22

Indra Devata

In Rig Veda Indra Devata has his own special importance. This can be gauged by the fact that Rishis of Rig Veda, 137 Rishis, i.e., 34% thought it necessary to express their views on Indra. Further, out of 1028 Suktas in Rig Veda, 314 Suktas, i.e., 30.5% have been offered to him. Besides this, dozens of Mantras have either been offered to him or he has been referred in them. A.A. Macdonell opines that none other Devata of Rig Veda has been given that importance and he is a "dear national deity".[1]

The list of some important Suktas offered to Indra Devata has been given in Appendix I. List of Mantras has not been given as it was quite lengthy.

A study of Rig Veda reveals that Rishis gave the greatest importance to five basic elements (Pancha-Tatva), viz., Aakaasha (Sky), Prithvi (Earth), Agni

[1]A.A. Macdonell, Vedic Mythology (in Hindi), Chaukhamba Vidya Bhawan, Varanasi, 1984, p. 102.

(Surya—Nuclear Fusion and other types of Agni), Vayu (Air) and Varuna (Water). Probably they thought that permutation and combination of these five basic elements are responsible not only for the creation of all material things, from moth to human beings, but also in providing them subsistence. So, each one of these basic elements was raised to the status of a deity and he has his own associates. For example, Vayu (Air) has Vaata Devata (hot air and water vapour), Parjanya Devata (clouds), Marudagan or Marut Devata (wind) and Apaam-Napaat Devata (lightning). In other words, one can venture to say that most of the Devatas (deities) of Rig Veda are natural phenomena. So, they are all powerful, omnipresent and omnipotent. One, who offers his or her prayers to them, i.e., obeys their rules, works in cooperation with them, does not overtax them and does not pollute them, derives the maximum benefits from them. He remains healthy and happy (this can be an interpretation of the meaning of Prayers).

Science seems to agree with most of the above mentioned things.

When, in the light of the above views, we examine Indra Devata, we are bound to get a little confused because we get his two pictures: one as a man and the other as a Devata. So, let us examine Indra Devata a little more closely.

Rishi Gratsamada Bhaargava Shaunak in Sukta 2.12 seems to reply who Indra is. In fifteen Mantras, he almost summarises all his virtues and activities. He says that he has done honour to the gods (it means he is superior and different than other gods), who has done extraordinary deeds as a Devata (deity) and without whom men do not conquer (battles). This confirms the impression that Indra had two roles—one as a human being and the other as a Devata (deity). Let us try to examine both.

I. INDRA AS A MAN

Rishi Kutsa Aangirasa says that Maghavan was the name of Indra (1.10.3.4). Rishi Vaamdeva Gautama calls him "son of strength" (4.24.1) or Maghavan. He had the features of a man. For example, he had a beautiful nose (6.30.6, 1.29.2), long-neck, large belly and strong arms (8.17.8), handsome jaw (8.66.4, 10.105.7) and moustaches and golden beard (10.105.7, 10.23.4). His own colour was golden (1.7.2), probably indicator of his radiant health.

This clearly indicates that Indra was a man. This is further confirmed by the following facts:

1. Indra was the leader of five tribes—Yadus, Turvashas, Druhyus, Anus and Purus (1.108.8). The references of five tribes have come at several places.

2. Indra was famous, both as a friend and as an enemy. A list of 58 friends and 70 enemies of Indra has been compiled from the Rig Veda. He fought innumerable battles with the enemies:

   (i) He seizes the treasures of the enemy (2.12.4, 5).

   (ii) Rishi Vasishtha prays him to give wealth after snatching it from the enemy (7.28.4).

   (iii) Going to the battle, desiring the spoil, he set himself to the acquisition of all (wealth) (19.99.3).

The list of battles can be multiplied: 1.102.4, 4.16.9, 4.24.1, 4.32.6, 7, 6.33.4, 6.44.18, 6.45.11, 12, 7.25.2, 8.3.9, 8.40.6, etc.

No Devata (deity) is known to have such a large number of friends and enemies. Only a man, and that too a king or a leader of tribe, can have this distinction.

3. Indra has been repeatedly shown as donor of corn so much so that some Rishis pray him to donate a "*better quality*" corn and that too in an unlimited quantity (5.39.2, 3), others demand "*excellent food*" (6.47.9) and some others food only (10.38.1). Even "*Strengthening food*" is demanded (6.60.12, 8.81.9). Devatas (deities) do not donate corn. It is a function of a man.

4. Not only corn is demanded, but there is no dearth of Rishis who pray Indra to give them cows and that too in good numbers (1.29.1, 1.51.3, 4.28.5, 4.49.4, 10.42.7, 10.47.1). Ilustrations can be multiplied.

   Rishis requested Indra either to protect their cows from enemies or give them cows after snatching them from enemies (6.17.1.3, 6.26.2).

   Certainly, these are not the doings of a deity. Only a man can do it.

5. Indra was called upon to donate horses and he obliged Rishis freely (1.29.1, 3.30.18, 4.32.17, 5.31.10, 6.60.12).

6. Indra donates other tame animals.

7. Indra donates houses (7.82.10, 7.84.4).

8. Indra donates even cities and Janpads (states) (7.18.3, 7.20.2, 10.48.8).
9. Indra donates wealth which is nothing else but yellow colour gold (8.33.3). Any number of Rishis pray Indra to give them wealth and he seems to oblige (1.53.1, 2, 3, 4, 5.39.1). Indra is shown freely donating wealth to those who are poor, who demand it from him and who are by his side (friends and not enemies) (2.12.6).

Besides the above mentioned human activities, Indra is also credited with a number of *social welfare activities.* A few illustrations are given below.

1. Indra released the glacier water (called cows in caves) (1.6.5, 6.17.6, 6.39.2, 6.43.3, 8.3.19, 8.14.8) collected at mountains in a circular form (Rishis call it Vrata which in Hindi means a circle) (5.30.5, 8.3.19) with the help of his Vajra and thus helped in formation of innumerable rivers. This water reached the sea. Indra is credited with releasing water in 99 rivers (10.104.8). King Bhagirath brought the Ganges to the plains and he became immortal. In comparison, Indra brought 99 rivers.

   Certainly, releasing waters in 99 rivers is no small an activity. It provided water to men, animals and fields and thereby helped men and agriculture.

2. Indra himself repaired (or got repaired) the banks of the rivers and thereby restored the flow of river waters. For example, Indra repaired the banks of the river *Parushni* so that the waters went to their former bed (7.10.9).

3. Indra turned the mighty river *Sindhu* towards the north (2.15.6). Probably, Indra changed the course of the river so that it may irrigate the areas which were not giving good yields.
4. Indra cleaned the rivers' beds from silt (Rishis call it Vrata), and repaired them (1.80.2, 1.32.6-10, 1.30.5, 3.33.6, 3.53.11, 4.17.7, 5.32.2, 6.17.12). Deepening the beds of rivers and repairing the pits was, probably, necessary to check floods. Certainly, this was a great welfare work.

All these activities, in the earliest period of humanity, go to show that Indra was a great man who was deeply wedded to the welfare of masses.

II. INDRA AS A DEVATA (DEITY)

We find that at a point of time, wise Rishis tried to make Indra, the man, a Devata. So, various efforts were made to show him, like other Devatas, a natural phenomenon. It appears the following efforts were made (in absence of the arrangement of Rishis in a chronological order, only a conjecture can be made of the sequence of efforts).

Phase I

1. Rishis pray: Indra may attain the Surya (Sun) (1.100.6).
2. Rishis equate Indra with Surya (Sun) (1.6.1, 1.33.10, 1.83.5, 1.121.6, 3.55.18, 8.89.1, 2).
3. Rishis declare that Indra created the Surya (Sun) (1.7.3, 1.32.4, 1.52.8, 2.11.18, 2.12.7, 3.32.8, 10.120.1).

   It shows no definite position could be assigned to Indra though several experiments were made.

Phase II

1. Indra, by description, it appears, was made the Red Colour Rays of the Surya (Sun). Indra's chariot and horses became of red colour (4.32.24). This must have been after Rishis had discovered the Red Colour Rays of the Surya and the necessity was felt to shift Indra from the place of Surya to some other place.

2. Indra was made the Usha (Orange Colour) Rays of the Surya (Sun) (1.7.2, 1.121.3). Either it was done to assign him a better place or there were some other reasons.

3. Indra was equated with the Green Colour Rays of the Surya (Sun). The colour of his beard and moustaches goes green (10.105.7). His nose becomes green (6.29.5, 6). His chariot and horses are shown green (3.30.2).

   In these three positions also, Indra remained associated with Surya Devata.

Phase III

It appears Rishis, in course of time, discovered the cause of rainfall. They found out that Vaata Devata (dry hot air and water-vapours) goes up. As they move up, they come in touch with the sphere called by Science as Troposphere (upto 10 miles above the Earth). This sphere is cool and so the water-vapours are converted into Parjanya (clouds). Marudagan (winds) move these clouds which have tiny water drops mounted on particles of matter. When these tiny water clouds collide with each other they join and become bigger and heavier water drops. After a particular stage the rain starts falling. So, wise Rishis found out what they were searching—a natural phenomenon. There was no Devata (deity) or known natural phenomenon who controlled rainfall. So, Indra was permanently made the *Devata of Rainfall*—a natural phenomenon, where he is still staying. The author thinks it will not be wrong to equate troposphere and what scriptures call *Indra-Loka*.

ANCIENT DEVATA

It appears after making Indra a Devata, efforts were made to show that he is an ancient deity. 68 Mantras of Rig Veda directly or through inference say so. For example:

Rishi Naudha Gautam calls Indra "*the ancient lord*" (1.61.2). Rishi Gautam requests "*Maghavan—be not different (from what you have hitherto been)*" (1.82.1). Same ideas were expressed in 2.17.1, 2.30.4, 3.31.19, 3.36.2, 3.42.9, 3.52.4, 4.16.21, 4.22.11, 4.25.11, 10.54.3, 10.27.7.

Now the question is: why Rishis tried to show Indra as an ancient god when the fact is, as the above study shows, Indra was a man and he was later raised to godhood. Several experiments were made to make him, like other gods, a natural phenomenon and ultimately he was made the *God of Rainfall*. So, why these efforts to prove that he was an ancient god?

Scholars should try to answer this question. The author's own feeling is that Rishis, by making Indra an ancient god, were trying to cement the idea that like other natural phenomena, Indra was also a natural phenomenon from the earliest times but this fact was discovered at a later stage.

CONCLUSION

The study of *Indra* reveals that Rishis of Rig Veda incidentally propounded a unique theory, which today is known as *Karma-Theory,* i.e., Action Theory. This theory like Newton's Third Law (in physical sphere) says *that man, in social life, will get reward for his each and every action. His good actions will give him good results and bad actions, bad results. The result of good and bad actions will not cancel each other.* Further, if a man is always doing good deeds, he may attain *Devatya* (Godhood). Conversely, if he is persistently doing bad deeds, he may become a *Rakshas* (Devil). This *Karma-Theory* was later explained by Lord Krishna to Prince Warrior, Arjuna (Mahabharat) in Geeta.

It appears Indra, a man, due to his extra-ordinary good deeds was raised to *Devatya* (God-hood).

In Rig Veda, Indra is not the only person who attained *Devatya* (Godhood). There are other illustrations also though they are not that much marked. For example, several Rishis, because of their good deeds including unmatched scholarship, were raised to godhood. Like other Devatas, Mantras of Rig Veda have been offered to them also. Some illustrations are:

S. No.	*Rishi*	*Mantras*
1.	Atri	5.40.6-9
2.	Kapinjal (Like Indra)	2.42, 2.43
3.	Vaamdeva	4.26.1-3
4.	Vasishtha	7.33.10-14
5.	Vishwaamitra	3.33.4, 3.33.8-10

Thus, one can conclude, by agreeing with A.A. Macdonell, that *Indra* is a "*Dear National Deity*".

APPENDIX I

List of some Suktas offered to Indra

Suktas

1.4, 1.5, 1.7.1-11, 1.16, 1.32, 1.33, 1.51-57, 1.61, 1.63, 1.80-84, 1.100-104, 1.130, 1.131, 1.133, 1.169, 1.170, 1.173-178

2.11, 2.22

3.30, 3.32, 3.34, 3.52

4.16, 4.17, 4.19, 4.22, 4.24, 4.29, 4.31

5.32, 5.39

6.17, 6.20, 6.22, 6.26, 6.29, 6.44, 6.46

7.19, 7.32

8.12, 8.17, 8.32, 8.34, 8.49, 8.53, 8.61, 8.62, 8.64-66, 8.70, 8.76, 8.78, 8.81, 8.82, 8.88, 8.92, 8.97, 8.99

10.22, 10.23, 10.27, 10.29, 10.38, 10.42, 10.44, 10.54, 10.55, 10.73, 10.74, 10.86, 10.99, 10.104, 10.105, 10.111, 10.113, 10.116, 10.120, 10.133, 10.134, 10.138, 10.144, 10.147, 10.148, 10.152, 10.153, 10.160, 10.171, 10.179, 10.180.

BOOK IV

On Summing Up

Deities of Rig Veda

— Natural Phenomena Deities

— Deities connected with Soul

— Man raised to Godhood

— Other Deities

— What prayers mean?

More views about Rig Veda

— Is Rig Veda a history?

— Conflicting views in Rig Veda

— Need for more Vedic Indices

— Need to arrange Rishis in a chronological order

Chapter 23

On Summing Up

The study of Rig Veda gives several interesting and important ideas. Some of them are discussed below.

(I) TYPES OF GODS

We find the following types of Devatas in Rig Veda.

1. NATURAL PHENOMENA DEITIES

Rishis of Rig Veda came out with the thesis that there are five basic elements—Surya (Agni), Aakaasha (Sky), Prithvi (Earth), Vayu (Air) and Varuna (Water). The permutation and combination of these five basic elements are responsible for the creation of all the material or worldly things and also their subsistences. The wise Rishis made these basic elements the main Devatas. All these five basic elements are natural phenomena also.

The studies of these main Devatas or the basic elements revealed to the Rishis that each one of them has also important sub-elements, or sub-natural phenomena. For example, studies of Surya Devata led them to ask: from where he gets light and heat? The answer was that in the core part of the Sun, called Photosphere (by science), continuous nuclear fusion is taking place which is giving heat and light to the Sun. Rishis found out gradually *Mata Aditi* (Photosphere), *Mausi Diti* (Chromosphere), *Surya-Sarparagyi* (Nuclear Fusion), *Dadhikra* (Photon), *Ashvino* (Two Bands of energy waves coming from Photosphere but which cannot be seen by the naked eyes on the earth), *Suryaa* (the middle Energy waves Band coming from the Sun) and Aadityaas (Seven colour Energy Waves of the Middle Band called Suryaa)—*Mitra* (Red colour ray), *Usha* (Orange colour ray), *Savita* (Yellow colour ray), *Bhaga* (Green colour ray), *Aryaman*, *Daksha* and *Ansha* (Blue, Indigo and Violet colour rays). All these sub-natural phenomena of the Sun were also assigned the status of Devatas. We can all them associate Devatas of the Surya Devata.

Similarly, the studies of *Vayu* (Air) by the Rishis helped them to discover a number of sub-natural phenomena connected with Vayu. They called them *Vaata* (Water-vapour and warm dry-air), *Marudagan* (Moving air columns at different heights called winds), Parjanya (Clouds) and Apaam-Napaat (Sky lightning). These sub-natural phenomena associated with *Vayu* were also raised to godhood.

In this way the five basic elements, or the five main natural phenomena and their associate sub-natural phenomena become 33 Devatas in Rig Veda.

2. VARIOUS PARTS AND PRODUCTS OF NATURAL PHENOMENA ALSO BECOME DEVATAS

Wise Rishis of Rig Veda, in their wisdom, started calling the important parts and even by-products of these natural phenomena Devatas. Probably, it was done because of their utility to man. For example, parts of Prithvi—mountains, sub- mountains, hillocks, important places were raised to godhood. This idea continued even in post Rig Vedic period. So, today we call Himalayas and Govardhan as Devatas, Rameshwaram, Dwarka, Jaggannath, Badrinath, Varanasi, Priyaga (Allahabad), Ayodhya, Mathura and dozens of places Devatas or highly sacred places.

Take another example, Varuna (water) is a main natural phenomenon. Its oceans, rivers and tanks were made sacred and Devatas. Ganga, Jamuna, Saraswati (invisible now), Pushkar (near Ajmer) are some examples. Today, the list has become longer.

Not only the parts but also the by-products of these main natural phenomena have been called Devatas. Here are a few illustrations.

(a) Animals, birds and aquatic animals have been made Devatas such as *Gaava* (Cow—6.28.1, 8.101.15), *Vrashabha* (Bull—10.102), *Ashva* (Horse—1.162, 1.163, 6.65.7), *Shain* (A Bird—4.26.4-7) and *Mandook* (Frog—7.103). Today, more animals, birds and aquatic animals have been added to this list.

(b) Vegetation has been made Devatas like Soma (full Ninth Mandal has been devoted to it). Today, *Pipal*, *Bar* (Banyan), *Tulsi*, *Kela* (Banana), and a host of other vegetations have become sacred and raised to semi-godhood.

3. SPIRITUAL GODS AND CRAFTSMEN GODS

With time three questions, it appears, drew the attention of the Rishis of Rig Veda:

(i) Why all the living beings, vegetations, birds, animals and even men become lifeless? We call them dead. What makes them dead? The studies revealed one more truth to Rishis. They found out a tiny, invisible weightless element, which they called SPIRIT. It is something like the modern electricity or energy or current. Just as electricity keeps a bulb burning, similarly, this invisible Spirit keeps all the living beings alive. These wise Rishis tried to search out the source of the Spirit. They found out that like a Power Generating Centre, a centre exists from where Spirits originate. They called this energy generating centre god *Vishnu*? They also found out a person, who is responsible to make the dead structures or forms alive by inserting this tiny Soul or Spirit in them. They named him as god *Brahamma*. They also found out the person who, after a period of time, takes out from the body this tiny Soul or Spirit and thus makes the living dead. They called him *Rudra* or *Shiva*.

Thus, they discussed three spiritual gods—Vishnu, Brahamma and Rudra.

(ii) The next question that arose was: There are the five basic elements—*Aakaasha* (Sky), *Prithvi* (Earth), *Vayu* (Air), *Varuna* (Water) and *Agni* (Fire) whose permutations and combinations can help in making various structures or forms. There is Soul to make the material structures alive. But where is the person who combines these basic elements and creates various structures? Searches led them to discover three god Craftsmen. They named them as *Vishvakarma, Tvashta* and *Ribhugan*.

(iii) When the tiny soul particle is taken out of the body or structures of all the living beings what happens to them. The Rishis found out that they are taken to a region in *Aakaasha*, called *Yama Loka*, by a god, whom they called King Yama. Thus, they discovered four Spiritual gods and three Craftsmen gods.

4. MAN RAISED TO THE STATUS OF GODHOOD

The Rishis of Rig Veda wanted that people should know the laws of nature, or each natural phenomenon, respect these rules or laws and observe these rules religiously, i.e., work in co-operation with nature and do not try to exploit or pollute nature. This, they thought, is in man's own interest. To popularise this idea, they propounded the famous theory of *Karma*, i.e., Action Theory. They said that man will be rewarded or punished for each of his good or bad action. These actions will not be cancelled by each other. One will have to bear reward or punishment of each action individually in this life or in the successive lives. This important theory was to keep people on the right track. This theory was made a part of *Dharma*. It was said that because of the persistent good actions one can achieve goodhood or even *Moksha*, i.e., salvation from the cycle of birth and death. To convince people of the truth of this theory, several examples were given by the Rishis in Rig Veda. Here only two examples are being cited.

a. Reading of Rig Veda shows that Indra, to begin with, was a man. He had features of a man. He had a father. He was head of five tribes. He had a large number of friends and enemies. He fought several battles and won them. He fought battles even for the friends sake. Besides this, he was devoted to humanitarian works. For example, he released cows kept captive in "mountain caves". In fact, it meant releasing accumulated, glacier waters in rivers. He was instrumental in releasing water in 99 rivers beds. He repaired rivers banks and removed silt from the beds of rivers. He even diverted the course of mighty river Sindhu probably to irrigate the barren lands and make them fertile. So, Indra was raised to godhood. He was made a *Devata*. Rishis, naturally, wanted to give him a place, like other *Devatas*, of a natural phenomenon. So, first he was equated with *Surya*, then made a *Surya*, then a *creator of Surya*. When these experiments did not work, he was made the Red Rays of the Surya, thereafter Orange Rays and Green Rays. Ultimately, he was settled as a Devata of Rainfall where he still stays.

b. The other example is of Rishis. Several Rishis, probably because of their good deeds and scholarship, were raised to godhood. Like other Devatas, Mantras have been offered to them also. Some illustrations are:

(i) Atri	5.40.6-9
(ii) Kapinjal (Like Indra)	2.42, 2.43

(iii) Sons of Mitratithi	10.33.6-9
(iv) Vaamdeva	4.26.1-3
(v) Vasishtha	7.33.10-14
(vi) Sons of Vasishtha	7.33.1-7
(vii) Vishwamitra	3.33.4, 3.33.8-10

(II) WHAT PRAYERS MEAN?

Almost all the Rishis of Rig Veda have prayed to their deities to give them one thing or the other. Mostly, corn, cow, horse, wealth, house, sons, etc. have been demanded. The prayers have also been made to Devatas to come, at the place of worship, and accept Soma. (Is it not personifying Devatas?) Not only this. Request has been made to bring other Devatas with them (for example, Agni Devata has been assigned this duty). And in a few cases, assistance to defeat the enemy has also been sought (Indra has been requested to do so).

Naturally, one will like to know that when wise Rishis, themselves, have raised natural phenomena and their sub-phenomena to the status of Devatas, then how can they think that they will be able to meet their above or other demands?

The author feels that if an Index of these demands is made itemwise, Rishi-wise and Devata-wise, then probably a better and more authentic explanation can be ventured. But till this is done, the author, on the basis of his studies, feels that the central idea behind these prayers was to convey people that if, like Rishis, laws of nature of every deity are followed, if respect and cooperation is offered to the deities and if no effort is made to pollute them and overtax them, then the kind-hearted and benevolent mother nature will bestow upon her followers health, wealth, longevity and give them able children. Their family life will become happy.

This seems to be the logic behind prayers.

In course of time the importance of the natural phenomena Devatas decreased and they were more and more personified. Besides this, new and more powerful Devatas appeared. For example, Vishnu, as the scriptures say, took birth in India in various forms. The most popular forms are of Rama and Krishna. Today they are important Devatas. The assistants of these Devatas are also called Devatas. Most popular among these Devatas is Hanuman, the monkey deity. These Devatas are, scriptures say, capable of appearing in person and granting prayers.

Thus, the very concept of prayers has gone a sea change.

(III) DOES RIG VEDA PROVIDE HISTORY?

There are two prominent views on Vedas, including Rig Veda. One is that Vedas are not the creation of men. Lord Brahma, the creator of the Universe, himself created Vedas. So, they cannot give history. Some scholars opine that the Rishis of Vedas pronounced what they saw. These Vedas are mainly prayers offered to various Devatas. Prayers cannot provide history.

The second view is that the scholars of the world have said that Vedas are repository of knowledge. They have not praised them because they have been created by the Lord Brahma or they are prayers. And the books of knowledge certainly can provide history.

THE MEANING OF HISTORY

History is a chronological record of events not confined to kings alone. It is a record of whole life of a country—Social, Political, Economic, Cultural, Religious, Science, Art, etc. The famous New Webster Dictionary defines it as "the branch of knowledge which deals with events that have already taken place; the study of investigations of the past; a narrative or account usually chronological of past events in the life of a nation, institution, or the like; anything that happened in the past. The sum total of past happening." Similar views are expressed in Oxford Dictionary. It says "Past events, methodical record of these",

Till this date neither the Rishis of Rig Veda nor what they said, have been arranged in a chronological order. And there are not many good Rig Veda Indices—Rishiwise, Deitywise, Topicwise, etc. In spite of these two great limitations, the author, after reading Rig Veda, with the help of translations, modern research methodologies and in the light of science, can venture to say that Rig Veda provides history. To substantiate this view, I am giving a few examples.

1. HISTORY OF VAJRA

A reading of Rig Veda gives a vivid history of Vajra, an instrument first used by Indra Devata for various purposes. I have tried to arrange the historical facts, in a chronological order, as under (this order may be wrong):

(a) Tvashta produced the first Vajra with the bones of Rishi Dadheechee (1.84.13). It was used to kill the enemy. It was made out of bones because no better material was available at that time.

(b) The next improved version was that Vajra was made of iron (1.81.40). It should have been possible to manufacture a Vajra of iron only after the discovery of metals and invention of Agni. By this time people should have learnt the art of melting iron and giving it a shape.

(c) Tvashta produced the improved version of Vajra, also to kill the enemy with the added quality that it produced loud sound (1.32.2, 1.61.8). Probably, like Gaandeeva bow of Arjuna it was to terrify the enemy. The Rishis of Rig Veda say so (1.52.7).

(d) The different types of Vajras were produced for different purposes:

  (i) Tvashta constructed a Vajra with thousand edges and hundred angles. Probably it was more manoeuvrable and so more effective.

  (ii) Vajra which could be thrown to hit the target.

  (iii) Vajra to remove rocks and stones of mountains. With the help of this Vajra the captive cow-water was released in rivers by Indra (10.104.8, 9). Thus, 99 river beds got water.

(iv) Vajra to remove silt from the beds of the rivers. Indra did it (1.32.8, 1.5.76, 3.33.6, 4.17.70, 6.17.12, 8.3.19).

(v) Vajra to divert the channel of mighty Sindhu (2.15.6).

(vi) Vajra to repair the banks of the river and fill in the pits (7.18.8, 9).

(e) Due to multi-purpose uses of Vajra, others also started producing them. It did not remain a monopoly of Tvashta or a monopoly of Indra (1.30.16, 1.63.2, 1.121.12).

Is it not history of Vajra?

2. HISTORY OF TRANSPORT

Rig Veda gives glimpses of various means of transport—road and water. By compiling them, an effort was made to guess the history of transport.

A. Road Transport

(i) Horse transport was an important one. In the beginning they were used for riding purposes. They were of different qualities such as Akra (1.143.7), Arvanta, Sapti, Vaajin (to carry load), etc. To increase the strength of the horses they were castrated (8.46.30).

Then, after some time, horses driven chariots were used. We find description of different types of chariots such as *Deerghapsas* (1.122.15) (long hands) and

Andi (1.35.6). Some chariots had two wheels (8.5.29) and some three wheels. They were called *Trichakra* (1.118.3). They were used to carry passengers and goods. They were also used in wars.

(ii) Bullock driven carts formed another important means of transport. It appears, in the beginning, even cows were used to pull the cart. Carts were of different types such as *Anas* (3.53.18), *Anadvaaha* (4.85.11) etc. They carried men and materials.

(iii) Camel was called *Ushtra* (1.138.2, 6.22.31). They were also used as a means of road transport. They were used both for carrying people and load.

(iv) Donkeys called *Gardabha* (3.53.22) were another means of transport. Its cross breed with horse was considered better and stronger than both. It was called *Ashvatar* and the cart drawn by it was known as *Ashvatari Rath*. They were used for both passenger and goods transportation.

B. Water Transport

In course of time, boat transport became increasingly popular. In the beginning, they were used to cross the rivers. After some time boats were used to navigate in the sea also. We find description of a varieties of boats such as:

Duman—small boat (8.19.14)

Draun—medium boat (6.2.8)

Navaa—medium boat (1.97.8)

Nau—medium boats (1.31.2)

Hundred oared ships which were very big (1.116.5).

This description reveals the status, types and quality of road and water transport at the time of Rig Veda. Certainly, it is history.

3. HISTORY OF ECONOMIC DEVELOPMENT

Rig Veda gives glimpses of the following stages of Economic Development (using economist F. List classification).

(I) Pastoral Stage

Description is found of cows, bullocks, horses, sheeps, goats, donkeys etc. Details are found about each of them. For example we find mention of *Gauri cow* who was a wild animal. It was caught and tamed (1.84.10, 4.12.6, 9.12.3). Vivid descriptions are found of *Goshta* (1.191.4), where cows were kept, *Gopa* (1.164.21), who took cows to jungle, various uses of milk and milk products.

(II) Agriculture Stage

We find mention of different types of lands such as jungle (*Aranya*) (1.163.1), sandy (*Dhanvan*) (3.45.1), barren (*Aartanaa*) (1.127.6), fertile (*Khila*) (1.127.6, 10.106.2), orchards etc. Names are given of persons who were engaged in different agricultural operations such as *Keenaasha* (4.57.8), *Dhanyaakrita* (10.94.13), *Veenaar* (10.106.10). We find several implements used for cultivation such as *Laangal* (4.57.4), *Vrika* (1.117.21), *Seer* (4.57.8), *Khanijo* (1.179.6), *Daatra* (8.78.10), *Tejan* (to measure land—1.110.5) etc. We find mention of different types of irrigation methods.

a. Well irrigation

Koopa (well—1.105.17), *Utsa* (10.30.8), *Avat*, *Khanitrim* (7.49.2), *Kaata* (1.106.6).

b. Canal irrigation—3.33.12, 3.45.3.

c. River irrigation—Inferences can be draw from 2.15.6, 6.17.12, 8.3.19, 10.104.8.

Different crops were grown such as *Yava* (1.23.15), *Vrihi* (5.53.13), *Chanas* (1.3.6), *Ikshu*, *Dhaanaa* (1.16.2), *Dhaanya* (6.13.4).

All this convincingly shows that agriculture stage was there in Rig Veda.

(III) Industrial Stage

We find description or mention of a varieties of industries such as:

A. Textile Industry

(i) Various cotton clothes—5.54.11, 8.7.25, 1.140.9, 9.69.5, 1.25.3, 10.136.2.

(ii) Woollen clothes—1.34.1, 1.113.4, 8.3.24, 10.85.29.

(iii) Stitched clothes—2.36, 1.92.4.

(iv) Other clothes—1.95.7.

B. Ornament Industry

(i) Ornaments of ears—8.78.3.

(ii) Ornaments of feet—5.54.11.

(iii) Ornaments of hand—1.168.3.

(iv) Ornaments of arm—1.166.9.

(v) Ornaments of ladies—10.85.6.

This shows that the art of mining gold, silver and various precious stones was there.

C. Utensil Industry

Names of about 17 utensils, made of different metals, woods, etc. have been given in Rig Veda.

D. Musical Instruments

Names of six instruments are found. They are *Aa-Ghaati* (10.146.2), *Karkari* (2.43.3), *Gargor* (9.69.9), *Gaudha* (8.69.8), *Dundubhi* (1.28.5), *Naadi* (10.135.7).

E. War Weapons

A long list of weapons such as stone weapons, cane weapons, bone weapons, iron weapons etc. can be compiled from the Rig Veda.

(IV) Commercial Stage

When all the ingredients of commerce and trade were available—agriculture, industry, transport, money unit, weights and measurements, then naturally there was commerce and trade also. Businessmen were called *Vanika* (1.112.11), value or price of goods was called *Vasna* (4.24.9) or *Shulka* (7.82.6), the coin was called *Nishka* (1.176.2) and the weight to weigh corn etc. was called *Isthivi* (10.68.3).

This brief description gives the history of economic development during the Rig Veda period.

To sum up, it can be stated that the above description should convince anybody that Rig Veda provides important landmarks of history of Rig Vedic period. The need is to search it with the help of research methods and an open mind.

Prof. M.G. Bakare, in his book *Hindu Economics*, has stated that Hindu scriptures, including Rig Veda, have enunciated several important postulates of economic life to promote real human happiness (individual, family, country and the world). Some of the important ones (taking family as a unit and not an individual) are:

(a) Abundance is desirable and not opulence.

(b) Competition and that too healthy is desirable.

(c) Small is the beautiful—small farms, small crafts, small families, etc.

(d) "Self-employment" in the family's economic activity is desirable than service of the others.

(e) Population control is desirable but by moral means, etc. etc.

The author's own studies of Rig Veda have confirmed Prof. Bakare's view.

(IV) CONFLICTING VIEWS IN RIG VEDA

A careful reading of Rig Veda vividly demonstrates that the views of different Rishis are not always identical on every point. For example:

1. *Usha Devi* is not called an *Aaditya* by majority of Rishis

while other Rishis, through inference, say she is also an *Aaditya.*

2. Nowhere the colour of *Bhaga Devata* (Energy Ray) is given. One will have to make a conjecture and conjectures differ because the views of Rishis differ.

3. One Rishi says that *Surya* is an *Aaditya* but others do not subscribe to this view.

4. One Rishi says that *Usha* is the daughter of *Surya* while others say she is the wife of Surya.

5. One Rishi says that *Usha* and *Night* are sisters but the other Rishi says that they are rivals.

6. Some Rishis opine that *Aakaasha* is the child of *Surya* and one Rishi says that *Aakaasha* is the father of all deities.

Such instances can be multiplied. These conflicting views are because the matter has not been arranged in a chronological order. These conflicting views simply may show the different stages of development of ideas.

(V) NEED FOR MORE INDICES

At present there is no Index on Rig Veda alone. And the Indices of words that are available are not exhaustive. Moreover, there are no Indices Rishiwise or Devatawise. With these limitations, more indepth studies of Rig Veda, on any particular topic, become very difficult. It is high time that honest efforts are made to produce different types of Rig Veda Indices—Rishiwise, Devatawise, Topicwise, etc.

(VI) NEED TO ARRANGE RISHIS CHRONOLOGICALLY

For a proper and scientific study of Rig Veda it is essential that Rishis of Rig Veda are arranged in a chronological order so that the views of Rishis get automatically arranged in a chronological order. This will facilitate a proper understanding of any topic of Rig Veda. This will also remove doubts or unnecessary controversies.

Bibliography

Rig Veda

1. H.H. Wilson, *Rig Veda Samhita,* Vol. 1-IV (Translation), Parimal Publications, Delhi, 2001 (In English).
2. Ralph T.H. Griffith, *The Hymns of the Rig Veda* (Translation), Motilal Banarsidas Publishers Pvt. Ltd., Delhi, 1999 (In English).
3. Pt. Shri Ram Sharma, *Rig Veda,* Vol. 1-IV, Sanskriti Sansthan, Bareilly, 1993 (In Hindi).
4. Maharshi Dayananda Saraswati, *Rig Veda,* Vol. I-V, Arya Pratinidhi Sabha (In Hindi), New Delhi, 2000.
5. N.S. Sontakke & C.G. Kashikar, *Rig Veda Samhita,* Vol. I-V, Vaidika Samsodhan Mandal, Poona, 1951.

Others

1. A.A. Macdonell, *Vedic Mythology,* Chaukhamba Vidya Bhawan, Varanasi, 1984 (In Hindi).
2. A. A. Macdonell & A.B. Keith, *Vedic Index,* Vol. 1 & II, Motilal Banarsidas Publishers Pvt. Ltd., Delhi, 1995 (In English & Hindi).

3. Dr. Surya Kanta, *Vedic Deva-shastra*, Shri Bharat Bharti (P) Ltd., Delhi, 1967 (In Hindi).
4. Dr. S.S. Gupta, *A Study of God Indra*, Krishna Publishers, New Delhi, 2001 (In English).
5. Bloomfield, M., *Contributions to the Interpretation of the Vedas,* in JAOS XV 143-63 (1893) (In English).
6. Bloomfield, M., *The Religion of the Vedas*, New York, 1908 (In English).
7. Keith, A.B., *Religion and Philosophy of Vedas* (In English).
8. Keith, A.B., *Some Modern Theories of Religion and the Veda*, in JRAS, 1907 (In English).
9. Max Muller, *Rig Veda*, Chaukhamba Vidya Bhawan, Varanasi.
10. Maharshi Dayananda Saraswati, *Rig Veda Bhashya Bhoomika* (In Hindi), Arya Sahitya Prachar Trust, Delhi, 1999.
11. Baldeva Upadhyai, *Rig Veda Bhashya Bhoomika*, Banaras, 1934 (In Hindi).
12. Lala Ram Pal, *Rig Veda Me Prayukta Vyavasaaik Shabdawali Ka Adhyan*, 1991 (Ph.D. Thesis).
13. Raj Kumar & G.L. Mittal, *Nootan Physics*, Vol. I & II, Naveen Publications, Meerut, 1990.
14. Reader's Digest, *Family Guide to NATURE*, Reader's Digest Services P. Ltd., N.S.W., 1984.

Dictionaries

15. Amar Singh, *Amar Kosh*, Nirnaya Sagar, Bombay, 1915.
16. Jay Shankar Joshi, *Halayudh Kosh*, Saraswati Bhawan, Varanasi, 1879 (In Sanskrit).